SAD DAD:

An Exploration of Postnatal Depression in Fathers

by

OLIVIA SPENCER

First published in 2014 by
Free Publishing Limited

Copyright © 2014 Free Publishing Limited

A CIP Catalogue of this book is available from
the British Library

ISBN: 978-1-85343-230-9

Typeset in Bembo 11pt by
www.chandlerbookdesign.co.uk

Printed and bound by CPI Group (UK) Ltd, Croydon, CR0 4YY

CONTENTS

CHAPTER ONE

Introduction

There is much cultural and medical conversation about postnatal depression and anyone who has had a baby will be familiar with the illness and might be aware of the warning signs. These symptoms (which are listed below), do not appear only in new mothers, but also in new fathers, yet they are rarely, if ever, discussed. When they are they are almost never classified as postnatal depression.

The *Diagnostic and Statistical Manual of Mental Disorders* **(DSM-IV-TR)** defines maternal post-partum depression (PPD), also called postnatal depression (PND), as a major depressive episode with onset occurring within four weeks of delivery. The following symptoms, as well as other behaviours, may also be present in depressed, new fathers: a marked loss of interest in virtually all activities, significant weight loss or gain, insomnia or hypersomnia, psychomotor agitation or retardation, fatigue or loss of energy, feelings of worthlessness or guilt, diminished ability to think or concentrate, and recurrent thoughts of death (American Psychiatric Association, 2000). Because men do not always have the same symptoms, and the symptoms can come and go, there are no reliable and consistent criteria available to assess these new fathers, and so a father who is depressed will often be misunderstood and misdiagnosed.

Depression is often less apparent in men than in women. Depressed men tend to change their behaviour, avoiding social situations and becoming cynical, indecisive and irritable. Sometimes depressed men are desperate to get away from their new family unit and so they change their behaviour in order to avoid being at home, yet this sort of behaviour is rarely seen as a symptom of depression. For instance, most would see a man spending excessive amounts of time at work away from the family as fulfilling his need to be the breadwinner and support the family, when actually this could be an example of avoidance behaviour.

Similarly, depression can be overlooked as the cause for excessive alcohol consumption, drug use, extramarital affairs, and even violence – often there are other causes. With all new parents, loss of appetite, disturbed sleep and a lack of energy are all part and parcel of caring for a new baby, which makes it difficult to pinpoint these as symptoms of PND. With such a range of symptoms, all experienced differently by each sufferer, it can be difficult to accurately diagnose PND in both men *and* women.

Changes in a mother's hormones during the perinatal period are well documented, but changes in male hormones have also been recognised – Kim and Swain (2007) have noted five observations about male hormone fluctuation:

- First, male testosterone levels decrease during their partner's pregnancy and post-partum period. They can decrease by up to a third. Although in healthy males this lowering of testosterone could increase sensitivity to their children's needs – this can be (apart from the fact they love their child and want to be a good father) the reason why fathers respond to their babies' cries and how they are able to form a strong attachment with the child. In depressed men, the lowered testosterone level may also be a sign of depression.

- Second, there are higher levels of oestrogen found in men during the last month of their partner's pregnancy and in the immediate postnatal period. This fluctuation is not normally seen at any other time in a man's life, and. This higher level of oestrogen can help to explain how some fathers experience pregnancy-like symptoms, such as weight gain and nausea.

- Cortisol regulates the body's responses to stress, but the amount of cortisol in the body can increase in the weeks before the birth. This is understandable, since many fathers feel apprehensive before their partner gives birth, but the level drops immediately afterwards, and such dysregulation can have a negative, de-stabilising effect. Low levels of cortisol can make a person feel tired and weak – tiredness is to be expected with a new baby, but hormone fluctuations such as these can make it seem worse.

- A hormone called vasopressin, which affects the ability of the brain to plan and organise behaviour, decreases after birth. This has been associated with lower levels of aggression, in an evolutionary sense this would be aggression against other males, but clearly the arrival of a new baby should not be a time for aggression.

- Prolactin is best known for enabling mothers to produce milk, but also has many other functions in the human body. Levels in men usually increase during the perinatal period – increased prolactin is associated with decreased libido and erectile dysfunction in men, but this could also affect a new father's mood.

It is clear there are many factors, both situational and physiological, that can affect a father's mood during the perinatal period, and yet this is an aspect of parenting that is currently ignored or overlooked by many experts and parents. This book looks at the issue of PND from many perspectives to explore reasons why men are affected by it, how it affects them, and why is it different for men. I have been able to talk to several professionals who encounter fathers every day in a mental health or community setting – their differing views are represented here – but they do all agree on one thing, which is that postnatal depression in fathers *does* exist and that we must take steps to do something about it.

CHAPTER TWO

The evidence so far – a review of recent research and study

Paternal post- or perinatal depression (PPND), as we will discover, is not a new idea. Medical professionals, scientists and researchers have been aware of the condition for several years, and there have been studies carried out to examine its effects, its incidence, and other related issues – including what can be done to raise awareness and help these fathers. In this chapter, I will refer to the (relatively small) body of evidence and research articles I have come across, as I try to trace some concrete observations surrounding PPND.

1. What are the effects of PPND on children?

It is widely accepted that postnatal depression in mothers can have a profound effect on a baby – these effects can last a lifetime in some cases. A mother is usually the primary carer for their child – at least during the first year this is almost always the case – and so it is self-evident that something that affects the main carer will also affect the child. But what about fathers? Only a small number of fathers are primary carers in their child's early life, with the vast majority returning to work after the standard two weeks of paternity leave. So why would their depression affect their child, since, presumably, they have less influence and less involvement in their care?

Several studies have looked at the effects of PPND on children, with assessments at varying stages in their lives, ranging from three months to seven years, and their results do consistently show that PPND has a negative effect. The Avon Longitudinal Study of Parents and Children (Golding, Pembrey, and Jones, 2001) has enabled secondary studies to use the huge amount of data it collects in order to analyse and discuss many other areas, including paternal and maternal postnatal depression. The Avon Longitudinal Study is also known as 'children of the nineties' since it is a long-term health research project which was started in the early 1990s to look at patterns of health and illness and what causes them. It is a longitudinal birth cohort study, which means that it follows a group of people throughout their lives – it is the only such project worldwide. Part of its significance is its size – more than 14,000 pregnant women were recruited (in Bristol and the surrounding area) who were due to give birth between April 1991 and December 1992.

These 14,000 women, their children and their families have been involved ever since, meaning that a huge range of people have contributed to the study. The information has been collected in different ways, mainly through participants attending a clinic in order to give samples and allow measurements to be taken, but they have also filled out questionnaires on many different aspects of their lives to give the study answers to 400 million questions. The parts of the study looking at postnatal depression used data collected throughout the pregnancy and the childhood that follows, usually through questionnaires being sent to mothers and fathers at specific points during pregnancy and after the birth.

The Edinburgh Postnatal Depression Scale (EPDS) is used to identify mothers at risk from PND; mothers may well be familiar with this, since a visit from the health visitor when the baby is a week or so old usually includes a quick chat about PND. Often healthcare professionals will run through these questions as a matter of course in order to identify mothers at risk from PND and to point them in the direction of more help. The scale consists of ten questions designed to correspond to various symptoms of clinical depression, such as feelings of guilt, sleep disturbance, low energy, the inability to experience pleasure, and suicidal thoughts. In the Avon study the EPDS was employed differently to how it is used by Healthcare Professionals in a day to day setting, since it was used to assess mothers and fathers during pregnancy. It was also used when the baby was eight weeks old and again at twenty-one months post-birth.

The Edinburgh Postnatal Depression Scale is as follows. The questions should be answered according to how the subject has felt over the past week, not just how they feel today.

In the past 7 days:

1. I have been able to laugh and see the funny side of things
   a) As much as I always could
   b) Not quite as much now
   c) Definitely not so much now
   d) Not at all

2. I have looked forward with enjoyment to things
   a) As much as I ever did
   b) Rather less than I used to
   c) Definitely less than I used to
   d) Hardly at all

3. I have blamed myself unnecessarily when things went wrong
   a) Yes, most of this time
   b) Yes, some of the time
   c) Not very often
   d) No, never

4. I have been anxious or worried for no good reason
   a) No, not at all
   b) Hardly ever
   c) Yes, sometimes
   d) Yes, very often

5. I have felt scared or panicky for no good reason
   a) Yes, quite a lot
   b) Yes, sometimes
   c) No, not much
   d) No, not at all

6. Things have been getting on top of me
   a) Yes, most of the time I haven't been able to cope at all
   b) Yes, sometimes I haven't been coping as well as usual
   c) No, most of the time I have coped quite well
   d) No, I have been coping as well as ever

7. I have been so unhappy that I have had difficulty sleeping
   a) Yes, most of the time
   b) Yes, sometimes
   c) Not very often
   d) No, not at all

8. I have felt sad or miserable
   a) Yes, most of the time

b) Yes, quite often
c) Not very often
d) No, not at all

9. I have been so unhappy that I have been crying
   a) Yes, most of the time
   b) Yes, quite often
   c) Only occasionally
   d) No, never

10. The thought of harming myself has occurred to me
    a) Yes, quite often
    b) Sometimes
    c) Hardly ever
    d) Never

For questions 1, 2 and 4 – score a) 0, b) 1, c) 2, d) 3
For questions 3, 5, 6, 7, 8, 9 and 10 – score a) 3, b) 2, c) 1, d) 0
Possible depression is indicated by a score of 10 or more. It is advised that notice is always taken of the answer to item 10 (suicidal thoughts).

The Rutter Revised Preschool Scales (Elander and Rutter, 1996) was used to look at children's emotional and behavioural development at forty-two months (three and a half years). Again, this took the form of a questionnaire, – which was sent only to mothers, who had to look at statements describing a characteristic or behaviour, such as 'Is worried, worries about many things' or 'Fights with other children,' and give responses relating to the frequency of these things in their children. The possible answers are 'Yes, certainly,' 'Yes, sometimes,' and 'No.' The individual statements on this questionnaire can be put together to show three different 'scales' of problems – emotional problems, conduct problems, and hyperactivity. There is also a scale for more positive behaviour, and the problems and the non-problems are combined to give a total score.

Some children were tested again at age seven, using a questionnaire called the Development and Well-Being Assessment (Goodman, Ford, Richards, Gatward and Meltzer, 2000), which is completed by parents and teachers. It asks about certain psychiatric symptoms, requiring lots of detail about how exactly they affect a child's functioning. The results are then inputted into a computer and assessed by experienced clinical practitioners.

The results from these questionnaires suggest that both pre- and postnatal depression in fathers, as well as mothers, has a lasting effect on children. Children whose fathers have been depressed during the postnatal period are more at risk of having behavioural problems when assessed at both three and a half years and at seven years old. This is true after taking into account maternal depression and other factors which can also have an effect on a child's development – depression in fathers alone can be a cause of these problems. It was also found that the early months of a child's life are a particularly vulnerable time, since fathers who were depressed in the immediate post-natal period were more likely to have a child with behavioural problems in the future.

The research also suggests that boys are more susceptible to the effect of paternal depression than girls – no further research on this has been carried out in these studies, but this is certainly an interesting observation. Perhaps boys are particularly sensitive to the way their fathers parent them, since fathers are often involved differently with their sons, whether that is due to ingrained social expectations or other reasons. In contrast, maternal postnatal depression can lead to a higher incidence of behavioural and emotional problems in a child, regardless of the child's sex.

A report on the results from these questionnaires goes into particular discussion about the possible reasons why a father's postnatal depression could affect their child. First, it says, depression might affect the ways in which fathers interact with their children; a depressed father is likely to feel anxious, tired, sad and uninterested, and be unable to function normally, both psychologically and socially, and so early interactions with the child would be abnormal. Second, the report points out that depression in fathers could be linked to other factors, such as marital conflict, which, while not directly related to the new baby, would still have an effect on him or her, since marital conflict has been linked with behavioural problems in children in previous studies. Third, there could be genetic factors to take into account, which could have an effect on behaviour and emotional development.

Finally, the report does acknowledge the possibility that there is something in the infant's own behaviour during their first few weeks of life that has an effect on the parent and increases the parent's risk of depression. This is an interesting idea, but it would be very difficult to analyse an infant's behaviour so early on in life, since it will not be consistent or predictable. While this final point may be possible, results have shown that there is a clear link between paternal depression and childhood behavioural problems, and that the paternal depression occurs first.

2. The impact of PPND on a couple's relationship and the family

Of course, depression in any relationship will mean that a couple will probably have to work harder to stay together. What does it mean for a couple's relationship if one of them has postnatal depression? And what does is mean for the children? And how are paternal postnatal depression, marital conflict and adverse emotional and behavioural outcomes for children linked? I came across a couple of studies that have been carried out in order to address this, and I will refer to them and their findings here. One study looks at the association between depressed parents and the functioning of the child and the family; the other also addresses this but looks at the effect of *antenatal* depression as well.

(i) In the first study by Ramchandani et al. (2011), fathers were assessed via the EPDS once their baby was seven weeks old. They were then visited, as a family, when the child was three months old, and both parents were interviewed using the Structural Clinical Interview for DSM-IV – put simply, this was to identify those who were suffering with major depressive disorder. The EPDS was used again at this point to analyse, specifically, mood and behaviour over the previous seven days.

Fathers also answered questions to do with their own antisocial traits, using the Antisocial Personality Problems Scale: twenty statements were rated according to a scale where 0 = Not true, to 2 = Very true. They were also required to complete the Alcohol Use Disorders Identification Test (AUDIT), which consists of ten questions about things like alcohol consumption, drinking behaviour, and problems caused by alcohol. This was included because alcohol misuse is often seen in men who are depressed.

Couples were asked about their relationship according to the Dyadic Adjustment Scale (Spanier, 1976), which looks at four areas key to any healthy relationship: consensus, affectional expression, satisfaction, and cohesion. They were also asked how critical they thought their partner was of them, and how critical they were of their partner. They were also asked to rate, on a scale of 0 to 10, how confident they were that their relationship would succeed.

Lastly, infants' behaviour was assessed using the Infant Behaviour Questionnaire, which asks parents to note how often their baby displayed certain behaviours over the past seven days, rating things like activity level, smiling, laughter, and distress.

Perhaps not surprisingly, the study found that postnatal depression in fathers is linked to an increased risk of disharmony for partner relationships. Clearly, if one partner is depressed, it is going to have a negative effect on the relationship – but interestingly, this study found that the cause of most disharmony reported – by both men and women – was a lack of affection. Furthermore, this dissatisfaction about levels of affection in the relationship is reported by both men and women, even if both were affected by PND. In addition to unhappiness over lack of affection from their partners, fathers also reported higher levels of criticism in their relationship – probably the symptom of a couple adjusting to life with a new baby and learning to find their way. It should be noted, however, that perceived criticism in relationships is a key predictor of a negative outcome in a relationship over time. This part of the study tells us what we already know: that male PND can affect a relationship so badly that the relationship crumbles – yet another piece of evidence to force us to take it seriously.

The importance of the Ramchandani study lies with the fact that the study assesses the impact of a depressed father on the functioning of the family at such an early stage in the child's life. Many studies have already concluded that the first months (and years) of a child's life are of fundamental importance to their development, and so the discovery that fathers' depression can affect this, too, is of great value. Environmental changes affect infants, who are particularly sensitive to them during their first few months. Parental depression and marital conflict are both examples of things that could have an adverse effect on a child's environment. Alarmingly, if a child experiences the effects of adversities at this time this can be significant and the effects on the child can endure into adulthood, increasing the risk of mental health problems later in life.

A critical finding of this study is that both paternal depression *and* inter-parental conflict each mean an increased risk of behavioural problems in children – independently of each other. If they are each a risk without the other, then the risk for the child when the two are combined is quite concerning.

But how, exactly, does a depressed father or a relationship full of conflict affect a child? There are several possibilities. Depressed parents or parents who are in an unhappy relationship are likely to be distracted or preoccupied with their own mental health, their partner's mental health, or some dissatisfaction with their partner and their behaviour. This would mean that the parent is less focussed and so might be less able to identify and meet the needs and demands of a baby. Additionally, parents who feel dissatisfied, angry or sad may be less able to parent in the best way for their child. As seen in previous studies, this could be a contributing factor to behavioural problems seen later on in the child. Clearly, much can be learnt here.

(ii) The second study (Hanington, Heron, Stein, and Ramchandani, 2008) also looked at the links between paternal postnatal depression and marital conflict, although it also took into account *antenatal* depression in both mothers and fathers, and examined the effects it had on relationships

and children. Again, participants were assessed using the EPDS
– this time during week eighteen of the pregnancy and again
at eight months after the birth. At both times marital conflict
was also tested, using questions with a scale of answers ranging
from 'almost always' to 'never' – the questions were things like
'Do you get angry with your partner?' and 'Does your partner
listen to you when you talk about your feelings?' This enabled
two scores regarding 'affection' and 'aggression' to be put
together to give an overall score. – both at 18 weeks gestation
and 8 months after the birth. The children of these parents
were assessed at three and a half years using the Rutter
Revised Pre-school Scales, which have been outlined above.

I'd like to highlight the links that this second study found
between antenatal depression, antenatal marital conflict, and
adverse child behavioural outcomes. Interestingly, if a couple
was depressed during the antenatal period *and* they were
experiencing marital conflict, then the link between
depression and problems with their child actually *decreased*
slightly. This could mean that there are other reasons for
behavioural problems, if there are any, but it is certainly not
true in every case. However, both antenatal depression and
antenatal marital conflict (together or alone) are strong
indicators of behaviour problems at three and a half years. The
study found that the scores for marital conflict increased by
more than 50% between the antenatal and postnatal periods,
suggesting that a couple who are having relationship
difficulties during pregnancy will continue to have those
difficulties afterwards, and, quite understandably perhaps,
more couples will report marital disharmony after a child is
born even if they were not in difficulty beforehand.

This second study supports some research that gave rise to
the 'programming hypothesis.' This argues that the antenatal
environment can have 'long-lasting effects on offspring

development, the consequences of which may persist into adulthood' (Weinstock 1996; Gluckman et al. 2005; Levine 2005; Connor et al. 2005.

But how can things on the outside affect a baby inside its mother's womb? Surely that is a safe environment, barring anything that would affect a mother's physical health. There are several ways the antenatal environment can affect a child. First, a mother could experience high levels of stress during pregnancy – this could be because of arguments with the father, or because of worries about a depressed partner, or anxiety brought about by their own antenatal depression. It could also be down to stress at work, or the wider family, or pretty much anything – high levels of stress in the mother mean that the unborn baby is exposed to higher than average levels of stress hormones, potentially putting the child at risk and having a negative impact on the child's behaviour during the early stages of its life.

It is worth noting, also, that there could be an increased risk of domestic violence if there is marital conflict present – this is of course something that could have a physical effect on an unborn child, but there is evidence to suggest that it has other effects too, again, possibly lasting into adulthood.

Ultimately, the study highlights the need for further research into stress and its effects on a baby during the antenatal period, including what times during pregnancy it is most damaging. If this could be achieved then it would be easier to pinpoint who needs help and when.

3. Antenatal and postnatal concerns

Obviously, birth and pregnancy is something men will never have to go through. They know this from very early on in life

– it is typically a little girl who will stuff a pillow up her dress and pretend to "be like Mummy." But of course, men *do* go through pregnancy – and birth, too, in most cases – participating in both events, just not physically. With modern norms such as antenatal classes and appointments with consultants and midwives, men are much more involved emotionally than they perhaps were a century ago. Their attendance at these classes and meetings is mandatory for some couples – of course some do not attend, but the birth has certainly become something a father will be expected to participate in and know a lot about.

Worries about childbirth are therefore not limited to mothers. Understandably, fathers have concerns too, but sometimes these concerns can turn into deep anxiety, which can lead to depression during the pre- and postnatal periods. A study by Gawlik et al. published in 2014 looked at perinatal depression in fathers in Germany and also the links between it and concerns over childbirth.

Fathers were assessed using questionnaires similar to the EPDS and others mentioned in previous studies. Since there was no existing method of measuring birth concerns the study constructed one. It covered things such as worries about sudden and unexpected onset of labour and being to cope with it, the fear of letting their partner down, the worry that they will not be able to cope during labour, worries about seeing their partner in pain, passing out during delivery, being unconscious (!), having no purpose during delivery, being a disappointment to their partner and worries about being too late for the birth. The purpose of the study was to see how far these concerns influenced paternal depression during the pre- and postnatal periods.

The study found that the results of the birth concerns questionnaire were more valuable than results of prenatal

EPDS and similar tests for predicting paternal postnatal depression. This is surely very important, as it is another way that vulnerable and at-risk men can be identified. It follows that more needs to be done to adequately prepare fathers for birth; birth concerns can be addressed quite effectively, and this in turn will open up ways to prepare them for fatherhood.

The study claims that pregnancy-related anxiety should be regarded as a separate symptom to general anxiety, since, when isolated, it is a strong indicator of future perinatal depression in fathers. As seen above, this can have long-lasting effects on both a couple's relationship and a child, and so more needs to be done to encourage men to attend antenatal classes with their partners. In addition, more father-specific sessions providing information about the birth and dealing with a young baby would be beneficial. Perhaps these could be organised and run by male health care workers, and, eventually, be a part of routine prenatal care. This sort of support would also provide a basic screening tool to identify men who are most at risk of developing postnatal depression, allowing further preventative measures to be taken.

A study in Sweden carried out by Bergström et al. (2013) began with fathers who had already been identified as suffering from a fear of childbirth and looked at how antenatal education prevents this. Men were selected from fifteen different antenatal clinics and randomly allocated, with their partners, to one of two groups of twelve. In one group men were trained to coach their partners during labour through special breathing and relaxation techniques known as 'psychoprophylaxis.' The men in this group were also taught how to give a massage, promote relaxation and give emotional support to their partner during labour. They were also told about other techniques to practise at home. Men were encouraged to discuss their anxieties, as well as their own strategies for dealing with them, with others in the group. The second group received basic antenatal preparation but were given no information about coaching, breathing techniques, or relaxation – this was the standard care model offered in Sweden at the time.

Both groups had four two-hour sessions of antenatal education that began in the third trimester (after twenty-eight weeks of pregnancy), and one follow-up session within ten weeks of the birth. The participants were also assessed using the Wijma Delivery Experience Questionnaire (W-DEQ). This questionnaire was originally developed for mothers in order to assess fears before childbirth and again afterwards to measure how frightening the experience actually was. It was modified for this study to exclude any questions deemed irrelevant for men. Some questions on the W-DEQ include, 'How do you think you will feel during labour and delivery?' with responses ranging from 'extreme panic,' to 'no panic at all,' as well as, 'Have you during the last month had fantasies that your child will be injured during labour/delivery?' with answers ranging from 'never,' to 'very often.' Questions for after the birth included, 'Did you feel prepared for labour?' with answers ranging from 'well prepared' to 'very unprepared.'

Before birth, fathers were also assessed using the Cambridge Worry Scale, which, again, was initially developed in order to measure anxiety in pregnant women, but was altered in order to eliminate questions which are irrelevant for men. This covers topics such as, 'will I be able to be with my partner for the birth?' because men are often anxious that they won't make it to the delivery room in time to witness the birth or to help their partner.

The study found that the extra antenatal preparation, including psychoprophylactic techniques, massage, etc., meant that fathers with a fear of childbirth were less likely to experience their child's birth as frightening. Those men also felt more prepared than those who attended the standard antenatal education sessions. It is interesting to note that the psychoprophylaxis model of antenatal education is similar to cognitive behavioural therapy – for the treatment of anxiety – in that it provides a structured and focused intervention that allows the participant to imagine the feared situation (birth) and to acquire some techniques that will help them to cope with it.

In women, fear of childbirth is known to affect the childbirth experience, but it is also linked to depression. This could also be true for fathers who have a fear of childbirth, as it is true that some of the men who participated in the study also reported feelings (in the antenatal period) of worry, low self-rated health, and negative feelings about becoming a father.

It is seen the norm in most Western countries in the twenty-first century for men to be present at their child's birth and yet most of the time they are given no guidelines as to how, exactly, they can support their partners. This is a major failing of current antenatal education, leaving men unsure of what is expected of them and unable to offer help and support to their partners, despite their desire to do so.

4. Psychosocial factors associated with PPND

So far I have discussed birth concerns and partner relationships, which can predict or contribute to the incidence of PND in fathers, but there are many other factors that can affect fathers as well – these are psychosocial factors. 'Psychosocial' is a term that relates to someone's existence in a social environment, which includes their interaction with it, and their psychological development. It is a way of looking at social behaviour in individuals – behaviour that a person will not necessarily be aware of themselves. A Canadian study by Francine deMontigny et al. (2013) addresses this.

Participants were recruited from eight different areas of Québec in order to cover a wide range of habitats – rural, semi-rural, suburban, and city. This study was particularly interested in recruiting fathers whose partners were breastfeeding or had breastfed for a significant time, since this is the norm in Canada (Some 80% of mothers breastfeed in Canada, which is higher than in the UK where, at six months, 34% of mothers breastfed in 2010 – Source: Unicef). Babies ranged in age from eight to sixteen months, and fathers were given a home visit by a research assistant, who oversaw the completion of several, self-administered questionnaires, each taking about an hour to complete.

The EPDS was used to identify the presence of depression, and the Dyadic Adjustment Scale was used to assess the quality of the marital relationship. (These have both been used in studies mentioned above.) The participants were also given the Parent Expectations Survey (Reece, 1992), which measures how effective a mother or father thinks their own parenting is, with regards to their role as a parent, their child, and their interactions with their child. The Parenting Stress Index (Abidin, 1995) was used as a tool to measure parenting stress. It highlights three areas of stress: parenting distress, a difficult child, and a dysfunctional interaction between parent and child. There was also the Parental Involvement Questionnaire (Devault and Dubeau, 2012) made up of fifty-two statements about tasks performed by fathers with respect to their child, such as 'I put my child to bed at night' and 'I comfort my child when he or she cries' with possible answers ranging from "never" to "every day."

Social support was also measured on a scale ranging from 0 (no help available) to 5 (extremely helpful), with a list of people who may or may not have helped the family since the birth, including medical professionals, family, and friends.

The study found that there are three main factors that contribute to paternal post-partum depression: parenting distress, the quality of the parental relationship, and the perceived parenting efficacy. Many of these links, however, had already been established by other studies, but the findings of this study indicate that depression seems to remain, even after the post-partum period.

Previous studies mentioned have already associated a negative relationship between the mother and father with paternal depression in the post-partum months. (Ramchandani et al., 2011) However, the findings of this study indicate that depression seems to remain, even after the post-partum period. The study also found that fathers who were depressed were more likely to be suffering from higher levels of parenting distress and a lower sense of parenting efficacy. This link had already been identified but this study claims it is the first to link paternal depression to parenting efficacy.

There are some things to take into account with this study, such as the fact that participants were volunteers, and – it might be the case that fathers who chose to be involved had a more negative experience of the time after birth than the fathers who did not take part. Second, the study focused on the parents of breastfed babies. Breastfeeding is exclusively a mother's job, and so the parents of breastfed babies would have a very different experience of the postnatal period than those who were formula fed, or a combination of the two. It would be interesting to compare these results to a study of fathers whose partners were bottle feeding instead, since bottle feeding can give parents a shared role in feeding their child, which can influence the feelings of each parent and their attitudes and experiences after the birth.

There is also a concern where self-administered questionnaires are used, since fathers might want to answer in a certain way – a socially acceptable way – even if that is not really the truth. They are also dependent on how good a father is at reflecting on his own feelings and experiences. It is perhaps better for fathers to be assessed by an independent researcher who might have a better idea of where a father stands in relation to others.

So, after all these negatives, where does that leave fathers? As we saw in a previous study, the quality of the marital relationship is related to paternal depression, but it is difficult to tell which comes first – relationship problems or depression. Care and notice should be taken by healthcare professionals to encourage healthy communication between partners. It is interesting to note the link between depression and a father's perception of his parenting, since it highlights just how important good parenting is to fathers. Often fathers will experience difficulties in their interactions with their child, and will tend to think this is because of poor parenting skills, which highlights the need for professionals to provide support for this relationship. The study goes on to say that it would also be useful to help fathers recognise their own role in making decisions to do with their children in order to feel part of an effective parenting team.

5. What can be done?

Reading about the research that has been done regarding postnatal depression in fathers can make the future for sufferers and their children seem very bleak. However, without research to discover links between paternal depression, marital problems, and childhood behavioural problems, no one would have any idea of the significance of this problem, let alone *how* to address it.

In the UK, the NHS is focused on the mother and child during pregnancy and birth, and ignores the father and his mental well-being, which also has a huge impact on the family as a whole. Postnatal mental health assessments should perhaps be carried out on both parents, but this would, of course, place additional strain on an already strained service.

Although many mothers are visited by a health visitor in the weeks following the birth, in some areas of the UK the community services are so stretched that these checks are carried out over the phone. When mothers do come face to face with a health-care practitioner again it is typically at a crowded weigh-in centre, where they take their infant to be weighed regularly in the weeks and months after the birth. Often, they will only get to talk to a professional at these sessions if there is a concern over the baby's weight or overall health. A mother usually has to initiate a discussion about depression or how they are coping – it is not usually asked. This is surely a problem for women – who can feel isolated and out of their depth as a new mother – if there's no focus on mental health. Something needs to change in the way parental health is viewed after childbirth in order to include both parents.

It is also important to note that not everyone will be honest in answering the questions posed to them by health visitors and GPs regarding their mental health. Some people find it difficult to be honest with someone they don't know and trust, and, in the case of questioning over the telephone, body language, facial expression and other physical signs of anxiety will be missed. Women are at least aware of PND, and may be encouraged to ask a GP about it, even if it's not relevant to them, but men are notorious for their reluctance to visit a GP for any kind of ailment, let alone because of a prospective mental health problem.

Men do need to be educated and made aware of the difficulties they might experience after they become fathers though, so they know when there might be a problem. The responsibility does not solely lie with GPs to pick up on the problem – it has to work both ways – but the key time for health-care professionals to be working with men needs to be during their partner's pregnancy.

Some people think that a father must be cared for from the very beginning of pregnancy in the same way a mother is, since the baby will be receptive to the external environment, which usually includes both parents, well before it's born. A father's presence at the birth is the norm in the UK – but they need to be prepared for it in a different way to women. For those who believe that the father needs to develop the same bond and connection with their child that the mother does, the absence of this is seen to contribute to postnatal depression in fathers.

i) Reducing postnatal anxiety in fathers

An Australian study Tohotoa et al. (2012) looked at ways of reducing paternal postnatal anxiety to follow on from previous research, which has shown that parenting capacity can be adversely affected by anxiety and depression.

Expectant parents were sent an information letter about an Australian initiative to increase the duration of breastfeeding when they registered for antenatal classes, and participants were asked to complete a questionnaire, which included the Hospital Anxiety and Depression Scale (Zigmond and Snaith 1983).

The HADS is reproduced here:

1. I wake early then sleep badly for the rest of the night
2. I get very frightened or have panic attacks for apparently no reason at all
3. I feel miserable and sad
4. I feel anxious when I go out of the house on my own
5. I have lost interest in things
6. I get palpitations, or sensations of 'butterflies' in my stomach or chest
7. I have a good appetite
8. I feel scared and frightened
9. I feel life is not worth living
10. I still enjoy the things I used to
11. I am restless and can't keep still
12. I am more irritable than usual
13. I feel as if I have slowed down
14. Worrying thoughts constantly go through my mind

There are four possible responses: 'yes definitely,' 'yes sometimes,' 'no, not much,' and 'no, not at all.'

For all questions EXCEPT 7 and 10 the scores are as follows:

Yes definitely – 3

Yes sometimes – 2

No, not much – 1

No, not at all – 0

For items 7 and 10 the scoring is reversed. Questions 2, 4, 6, 8, 11, 12 and 14 reflect anxiety. Questions 1, 3, 5, 7, 9, 10 and 13 reflect depression. A score between 8 and 10 is considered a borderline case, and a score of 11 or more indicates a degree of anxiety or depression.

The fathers were split into two groups – the first participated in the usual antenatal classes, which addressed issues such as labour, birth, pain relief, and breastfeeding. The second group also attended the routine antenatal classes, but there was an additional hour of class incorporated into the standard programme. Crucially, this second group was taught by a male antenatal educator, who addressed three main topics: the role of the father, the importance and benefits of breastfeeding for both mother and baby, and what to expect in the first four weeks at home with a new baby. The fathers were also sent extra information for the first six weeks following the birth, about how to support their partner's breastfeeding, developmental milestones, ways to reduce stress, and postnatal depression.

All fathers were sent a second questionnaire when their baby was six weeks' old to gather information about the method of birth and any complications that may have arisen. It also asked about current feeding practice and repeated the HADS. Fathers in the second group were also asked to give their feedback on the six-week support package.

The study found that fathers in the second group (with extra antenatal and postnatal education and support) reported less anxiety from the initial test to the second postnatal test than the first group. Men with PND were still identified in both groups, and so this indicates that ante- and postnatal intervention like this will only help with paternal anxiety and not depression.

The study received very good feedback about its extra ante- and postnatal education and support, with almost all fathers giving positive responses about both the content and the facilitators. The fathers valued both the insight it gave them into how their role in the family would change after the birth, and the practical information about what they could actually *do* to help with the baby. The fathers were also very positive about having the classes run by another man, especially because he was a father too.

The main thing to take from this study is that this sort of intervention – and by that I mean the extra information and support provided to some fathers – is effective in reducing paternal anxiety in the perinatal period. Giving fathers extra information in the perinatal period in particular is probably of most value; information about the problems to expect with a newborn is not effective when given, for example, at school, or before a man is in a position to become a father, The same could, of course, be said of girls and women who are not ready to start a family.

It is also worth noting that although not commonplace in antenatal classes, topics such as stress management, lifestyle changes, and the discussion of increased strain on the marital relationship were all felt to be of value to men who took part in this study. This perhaps gives a good indication of the sort of information that should be available to men in the UK and worldwide. In particular, the provision of information by a man who is a father himself seems to be key. Men clearly need to talk to other men about the upcoming changes in their lives, and want to talk to other fathers and share experiences. At the very least, sessions that are solely for fathers could be useful, since most antenatal classes are aimed at mothers, thus alienating fathers and perhaps making it difficult for them to ask questions and see where they fit in.

ii) What can nurses do to help?

An article by Sherri Melrose in *Contemporary Nurse* (2010) gave a useful discussion of how nurses might begin to help fathers with post-partum depression. It discussed the pros and cons of using many of the questionnaires I've mentioned, as a tool to identify fathers at risk, but it also discussed a newer, male orientated one – the Gotland Male Depression Scale (Zierau et al., 2002). This comprises thirteen questions aimed exclusively at men and geared towards specifically masculine behaviours and symptoms of depression. Although easy to use and widely available, the questions don't specifically refer to the post-partum experience of a new father. However, as we will see later, depression in a new father is rarely identified as suffering from post-partum depression. The Gotland Male Depression Scale is reproduced here:

During the past month have you or others noticed that your behaviour has changed, and if so, in what way?
Possible answers for all items are:
Not at all – 0 points
To some extent – 1 point
Very true – 2 points
Extremely so – 3 points

1. Lower stress threshold/more stressed out than usual
2. More aggressive, outward-reacting, difficulties keeping self-control
3. Feeling of being burned out and empty
4. Constant, inexplicable tiredness
5. More irritable, restless, and frustrated
6. Difficulty making ordinary everyday decisions
7. Sleep problems: sleeping too much/too little or restlessly, difficulty falling asleep/waking up early
8. In the morning, especially, having a feeling of disquiet/anxiety/uneasiness
9. Overconsumption of alcohol and pills in order to achieve a calming and relaxing effect. Being hyperactive or blowing off steam by working hard and restlessly, jogging or other exercises, under- or overeating
10. Do you feel your behaviour has altered in such a way that neither you yourself, nor do others recognise you, and that you are difficult to deal with?

11. Have you ever felt or have others perceived you as being gloomy, negative, or characterised by a state of hopelessness in which everything looks bleak?

12. Have you or others noticed that you have a greater tendency for self-pity, to complain, or to seem 'pathetic'?

13. In your biological family is there any tendency towards abuse, depression/dejection, suicide attempts, or proneness to behaviour involving danger?

1-13 points – no signs of depression
13-26 points – depression possible
26-39 points – clear signs of depression

Questionnaires such as this one and the Edinburgh Postnatal Depression Scale are useful in identifying men at risk, none are specifically designed to measure postpartum depression in men. They can certainly give some insight into the way depressed men are feeling around the time they become fathers, but because there is limited knowledge about PPND as a whole, these questionnaires might not be appropriate screening tools. Since they are all that is available now though, nurses and other health-care professionals must use them.

Other than the use of questionnaires there are many other things – mostly to do with increasing awareness of PND and its symptoms – that nurses can do to help fathers. Nurses and health-care professionals who are not directly involved in childbirth and early child health can also increase public awareness of the condition. Nursing is a very sociable job where people of all generations are often seen during the working week. Any number of those people could be expecting a child somewhere in the family, and so information about PPND could be of use to a family member and could find its way back to the father affected.

There are already, the Melrose article claims, many outreach programmes in place directed towards new mothers, whether these are in the community through schools or in health clinics, and it would make sense to use the same channels to target new fathers. This sort of thing would also provide information about paternal post-partum depression, if they do not so already, and to reach new fathers. Existing programmes directed at mothers could also include information about PPND – mothers will notice the new father's behaviour and mood, or at least be alerted to it and whether it should be of any concern.

Quantifying a disorder, and providing facts about what is already known, and about how many people it affects, can help to reduce the stigma. Mental health disorders are often difficult for people to talk about or admit to, and so it is important to have information available so that it is more familiar and therefore potentially less shameful for sufferers. Professional literature, such as the studies I have looked at here, could be summarised or reproduced – whether you are a health-care professional or not – and shared with interested individuals.

There are so many other ways to get the information about PPND out into the wider world. Doctors' waiting rooms, hospital waiting areas, community buildings, nurseries and public libraries would all be ideal places for displaying information in the form of a poster. In terms of the EPDS or the Gotland Male Depression Scale – these could also be included on publicity material. Certain questions might grab someone's attention – a sufferer or their relative – and could be a useful way of sharing diagnostic symptoms and behaviour, and providing contact details for counselling services. Perhaps student nurses could use their assignments to create such posters and other promotional material; the idea of having their work viewed by the public could be a good motivator.

Nurses are encouraged to discuss the results of the questionnaire or scale they are using. The nurse, or whoever is carrying out the diagnostic questionnaire, can also take control and make a referral for further help right then and there, ensuring that more fathers get the treatment and help they so badly need. In extreme cases it can identify men who are having suicidal thoughts and are a serious risk to themselves – in these instances immediate help can be given.

Finally, it would help if nurses were aware of a mother's mental health history; a previous history of depression will mean there is a greater risk of developing PND, and early identification, besides from benefiting a mother, will also benefit a father, who is more likely to suffer PPND as a consequence.

As I have already mentioned, in most cases, men are far less likely than women to seek out counselling or therapy, which is why open acknowledgment and discussion of PPND is so important in the first place. Fathers may feel that they don't want to burden their partners with their problems, so mustn't be made to feel alone with their problems at every turn.

An Australian article (Habib, 2012) has similar ideas about ways to help fathers with PPND, but it acknowledges that there cannot be one 'cure' or focus suited to all sufferers. It suggests that there needs to be several levels of support provided so that all degrees of PPND can be recognised, addressed, and treated, and it goes through examples of these.

Level 1 would see that new and expectant fathers have information on parenting from the internet. This information would be specific to fathers, and it would discuss things such as managing work and family responsibilities, or keeping relationships healthy. Fathers would also be given information about depression, including symptoms to look out for and how to access help if they need it. This sort of resource would be freely available to all members of the public and all expectant parents would be made aware of it.

Level 2 could mean that information is made available at a seminar or education group, like an antenatal class, but aimed solely at fathers. Again, the aim would be to give fathers information to prepare them for parenthood, and to make them aware of the symptoms of PPND; however, in this setting, fathers who are at risk or showing early signs of the condition could be identified. It would also allow fathers to discuss whichever topics were concerning them, and, as previously noted, the opportunity for fathers to discuss issues with other fathers is of great value.

Level 3 would be for fathers who had been diagnosed with PPND (by means of a screening test and a clinical diagnosis) and would involve group treatment. These sessions could be structured to address ways to cope with the role of being a father, cope with stress, and cope with family relationships. Some sessions could also include the men's partners so that communication between them can be improved.

Level 4 is more serious and would offer support on a one-to-one basis. In some cases this might lead to a psychiatric assessment and medication as part of treatment.

It is suggested that all fathers are screened by a GP using the EPDS and the GMDS and so if PPND is diagnosed or hinted at the father can be pointed towards the most suitable level of treatment. All fathers would be told about the freely available, web-based information, as in level 1.

CHAPTER THREE

Angry men – a discussion
Adam Jukes

Adam Jukes is the founder and director of the Men's Centre in London where he works as a group analyst and analytic psychotherapist. It was Europe's first dedicated treatment centre for abusive men, but it also provides treatment for men with most other kinds of personal problems. Over the past twenty years he has published several books examining men's relationships with, and attitudes towards, women. The behaviour of men, and the reasons they behave the way they do are something like his 'specialist subject'. Through years of work he has encountered many men, with many problems, and he maintains that depression, not to mention *perinatal* depression, manifests itself very differently in men than in women, and it is this that we need to address more than anything else.

Jukes claims that every patient he sees has a history of depression, but since men are generally less self-reflective than women and less likely to go to a doctor, they may not have realised this. Men who are depressed tend to exhibit symptoms such as anxiety, sleeplessness, weight changes, manic episodes, and risky, self-destructive behaviour, such as adultery, gambling, or excessive drinking. This sort of thing is not uncommon; it's just that we don't always notice it enough to remark on it unless it happens to us. Jukes tells me about one patient in particular who was depressed; he was a married man with young children, who started seeing prostitutes. The father believed that the prostitutes were providing him with everything that his wife couldn't, and would see the same one for a while, but would then have to find another woman after a time because he'd 'fall in love'. . He would get to know them and they would tell him their story – sooner or later, his morals would get in the way. He would have learnt that many of them were very young, from damaged backgrounds, immigrants in a strange country – and he'd start to see them as people, thus rendering him unable to maintain the sexual objectification needed to have sex with them, and so he would have to find another prostitute, and the cycle would start again. In addition to seeing prostitutes, the man started drinking heavily and watching masses of porn on the internet, masturbating frequently. The man already had a history of all this sort stereotypically 'male' behaviour – it was not a cause for alarm when he was single and unmarried. – so no one remarked on it.

Even now, as a married father, the drinking, the porn, the anger and masturbation are all seen as typically male behaviour, and so, as is often the case, go under the radar. What was not seen behind all this 'maleness' is that he was completely split off, mentally, from his wife and children as if they were not there. This can ultimately be a strong indicator of depression in men, who are more likely than women to act out with risky, self-destructive behaviour.

Throwing himself into his work after his child was born was also something that Jukes' patient did. Work is seen as acceptable and necessary for me, so that even working overtime is not particularly controversial, since it can fulfil the traditional expectations of man as provider. If questioned, working overtime can be explained away, but in some cases a man might be finding it too difficult to be at home with a new baby – no longer a priority for his wife – and so escapes into the office with the pretence of fulfilling his role as provider for his family. This notion of 'escape' is also mentioned by Michel Odent , who talks about new fathers who take themselves away from the family unit after the birth – to work or to the golf course, or the computer game console – because they had to get away in order to protect themselves (see Chapter Six).

The expectations of fathers have changed significantly in the last fifty years or so, with post-feminism and what one might call the 'natural male response'. Social pressures now dictate that a father should be involved with childcare and housework as much as a mother. Fathers are expected to get up during the night with their newborn, taking it in turns with their partner, perhaps, and to help out with washing, cleaning, etc. The main pressure, says Jukes, is to be responsible. Fathers are expected to provide for the child, not only materially but also emotionally; there is a pressure to provide a protective environment for the mother and child unit.

So, while a father is often at work all day, they may come home to a highly educated, intelligent female, who may have once had as good a job as he; who is frustrated and angry after a day caring for a baby and using so little of her intellect. It is undeniably very difficult for a father to work all day and to come home and care for his child, since his partner is so often the primary carer and is more practised and knowledgeable than he.

This can produce feelings of anger in a father, since he cannot meet the expectations of his wife or society, despite going out to provide for them on a daily basis. Often, according to Jukes, feelings towards a new baby stem from one's own childhood – this is usually very complex, and many people don't realise these connections unless they have been through therapy or counselling, but these connections are a significant and useful way of understanding what happens to men after the birth of their children.

Jukes argues that some men experience conflicted feelings towards their baby because of unresolved conflicts with their own mother, and what occurs between a man and his baby is very similar to a sibling rivalry, since they are both competing for the affections of the same mother. He tells me about a booklet produced by his centre for abusive men, which addresses how such men might deal with their pregnant partners. Much domestic abuse begins during pregnancy, so a leaflet like this would hope to mitigate that by helping men identify some of the negative feelings that might be associated with it. One thing the leaflet highlights is the loss of the breast – the breast is a symbol of food, nourishment, comfort, and affection – and how they might feel when faced with the loss of such things that they may have been getting from their wives or partners. This reaction is dependent on a father's early relationship with his own mother – if this was a good relationship the sense of loss is mitigated and the father is able to delight in the presence of his child, which will bring about a positive association and there will be no jealousy.

Jukes says that men are bad at metabolising and dealing with disappointment; they don't always acknowledge it as something they are feeling – it's easier, and, therefore, more common, to just get angry and blame someone else for the situation. A man may get angry and blame his wife for not keeping the baby quiet at night, or for getting pregnant in the first place, but may never ask himself about the root of this rage. In facing the pain of disappointment, says Jukes, we are confronted with reality – things are not as we want them to be. Jukes talks about Melanie Klein, who suggests that we must reach a 'rapprochement' with the world. The world, according to Klein, will never be how we want it to be, but we must find ways of dealing with it and dealing with the pain. We must either re-evaluate our expectations and come to terms with the way things are, or we must make ourselves more effective in the world so we can shape situations to how we want them to be, without resorting to hostility, anger, murderousness or theft – which would be symptomatic of failing to reach this 'rapprochement.'

Jukes has experienced many patients who cannot articulate their disappointment. If they are asked what has made them angry they will never say that it is because they feel disappointed, but will instead lay the blame on the situation itself.

Jukes also talks about Freud and his paper 'Mourning and Melancholia' to give a deeper understanding of the anger and resentment some fathers feel towards their baby and their situation. The father has lost his old life, the object, and the part of his old life that he loved he identifies with and tries to become like it and recreate it so as not to lose it. But he still feels rage towards the thing he has lost, and so the superego (the part of our unconscious that controls our sense of right and wrong) takes the rage and becomes angry and strong, attacking the good parts of the thing that has been loved and lost. Everything in your life has been identified with what you have lost, and so you are left with only damaged things, or 'objects'. A person (in this case the father) then feels guilty about being angry with what he has lost, and this triggers depression.

This is part of Freud's theory in very basic terms – to put it in context, perhaps consider it like this: a new father feels sad that his life is no longer how it was before he and his partner had a baby, and so he tries to hold on to it by doing some of the things he used to do, such as playing golf all weekend, or working late. But he is still angry that he doesn't really have this kind of life any more, and this anger infiltrates everything, since everything is now associated with his new life as a father. He must always think of his child and partner when before he didn't have to, and so all the time he is feeling angry.

But the new father feels guilty that he is angry and that it is this situation that has made him angry (whether this is a conscious acknowledgement or not) and so he begins to feel more and more depressed about the whole thing. Jukes says this produces all sorts of problems for a man – he loves his partner, or he knows he *should* love her, and their union has produced a child (an object) and he knows he *should* love the child too; it is what is expected, and so when a man feels anything other than this, the guilt can be overwhelming.

Often these feelings are worse if the baby was unplanned – in the worst instance a man may feel conned by his partner, thinking she *made* him get her pregnant. This heightens the conflict between love, rage, and jealousy, at a time that is already known for being difficult for couples and their relationship. A first pregnancy and birth is the time when men are most likely to abuse their partner, and the time when some marriages start to fail, but this can also occur during a second or subsequent pregnancy.

In his book, *Is There a Cure for Masculinity?*, Jukes writes about a man who came to him after he was physically abusive towards his wife during her second pregnancy. His wife had given up her career as a teacher and as a consequence the man had to work harder to earn more money, while at the same time helping out more and more around the house. His wife, he said, had stopped cooking meals, wasn't interested in him or in sex, and was constantly berating him for his lack of contribution. He felt overwhelmingly that this was a terribly unfair situation, and would spend his session with Jukes complaining of his wife's inadequacy as a wife and mother, and had terrible and paranoid things to say about her and their two-year-old child, who he believed was colluding with her mother to get him out of the house.

Jukes was unable to help this man enough to make his presence at home acceptable for his wife and children, but he did continue to see him once he had moved out of his marital home and into his parents' house. Through further sessions, Jukes explored the man's history, and discovered that he had experienced an intense rivalry with his younger sister, feeling rejected by his mother – and then his new sister, as his bullying made her nervous towards him and unaffectionate. Jukes is sure that the man's wife represented his mother and his child the younger sister – this is an example of 'transference' – the unconscious projections of feelings onto other people. Jukes maintains that this transference is not unusual, but is very complex, and, almost certainly, this man would never have made these connections had it not been for the therapy he sought because of his violent behaviour.

It is clear in most people's minds that perinatal depression is, historically, a female problem. But what does masculinity and femininity have to do with being a parent? And what is the difference between men and women that makes this sort of depression apparently more common in women than men? Jukes says there are no essential differences. There has been lots of research into what makes a man a man and a woman and woman (apart from the very obvious physical attributes), but the fact is that men differ more from other men than they do from women. The same can be said of women, too, but if we want to explore masculinity and femininity, a look at behaviour is a good place to start.

Masculinity is what men *do*, often according to cultural expectations, and so it is easy to spot differences in men if you look at how they behave. When Jukes talks about how men deal with their anger following the birth of their children, it is an example of how men can be very poor at dealing with their emotions. Traditionally, men do not talk about their feelings; the idea of sharing innermost thoughts to a trusted friend might well be considered a 'girly' notion. Times are undoubtedly changing, but there will still be many men who feel awkward about admitting how they feel if it is not what is typically expected of them as men. Another example of changing times is the introduction of paternity leave within the last twenty years or so. Now a father is expected and often encouraged to take time off work to be at home with his partner and newborn baby, but, as mentioned, no thought is given to how men might feel during this period; the focus is generally on a mother and how she is coping, emotionally and physically.

Of course anxiety is something that affects both mothers and fathers: it is undeniably a very stressful time for both partners when a new baby arrives. Jukes suggests that women are probably better at dealing with anxiety than men, who, Jukes says, tend to act out in the same ways that depression might cause them to – by doing risky things and setting up dramas because they can't talk about their feelings. For instance, a man might begin sleeping with other women and become anxious that his wife will find out, but will continue, regardless, in order to avoid having to explain to himself why he feels like he doesn't want his new child or hates his wife.

Again, this is an example of a man, apparently unconsciously, creating a way to get out of his new situation as a father. Jukes sums this up with this statement: "the most common precipitant for divorce is the birth of the first child."

In his book *Is There a Cure for Masculinity?*, Jukes puts forward another reason for men choosing to act out, other than to alleviate extreme anxiety surrounding pregnancy and birth. He suggests that these sorts of behaviours enable a man to feel in control and hold on to an 'unravelling' sense of masculinity, bolstering his independence, toughness, and potency. A man may feel helpless when faced with the task of parenting, and there is little wonder that this is the case since so much advice and help is directed solely at mothers.

I asked Jukes how useful he thinks leaflets about domestic abuse are to men on the cusp of fatherhood. On the whole they would be useless, he says, and wouldn't be read. I can see how that would certainly be true until more men prioritised mental health as something to be aware of during the pre- and postnatal period. The fallout from abusive situations is extreme, so it would be dismissive, says Jukes, to say that leaflets would be a waste of time if it ultimately helped to prevent just one case of abuse. Jukes tells me about a project he set up some time ago to help men deal with the enormity of becoming fathers. So much work had been focused on the mother and child, and while important, it left out the other important figure in all of this – the father. He devoted much time to the project; writing papers, talking to ministers and the directors of locally-run organisations, and other charities – all of whom were very supportive and interested in the initiative. It was suggested that a structured programme of support group sessions could be run specifically for men about to become fathers for the first time. This would have enabled and encouraged men to face their feelings while their wives and partners were pregnant so that they could articulate what was going on for them emotionally which would help them to prepare for what they were going to have to deal with.

However, Juke's project was met with such strong resistance and disdain when they tried to get it off the ground – from both the people who would be running the sessions and from fathers who would have attended- that the project was abandoned. Jukes is adamant that this sort of system would have been cheap to run, since fathers themselves could have been trained to lead the sessions, while being able to refer any cases they couldn't deal with to the local mental health trust.

Would this be the kind of group new and prospective fathers would attend? Clearly, *something* needs to be done in communities and at that level – perhaps in the same sort of settings as women go to for similar classes. Antenatal classes, which often are directed at *couples,* could perhaps be encouraged to include fathers in more in what they cover, in addition to birth and the first few weeks. I feel it is unlikely to be something men would actively seek out. But, as discussed in other parts of this book, the research is there telling us that support groups for men are effective. Fathers may feel like they don't have time, or that they don't need any help and that a support group, or even *any* fathers group, isn't something 'conventional'. While it is clear that changes do need to be made, and funding needs to be secured in order to make those changes, this needs to be accompanied by a change in attitude in fathers themselves.

Jukes ultimately maintains that dealing with the anxiety and anger surrounding pregnancy and birth would be relatively easy – but the problem remains that men very rarely present themselves to GPs or other health-care professionals with the problem of paternal perinatal depression. Unfortunately, unless there is a change in the way outreach for mental health problems is seen, PPND will only present itself in the divorce courts. Work has to be put in by couples to engage in regular, honest dialogue in order to break the cycle of acting out, which may have become the default response to dealing with difficult emotions.

CHAPTER FOUR

Why do dads get depressed? A discussion with Barry Watt

Barry Watt is a psychoanalyst living in London. His work is less specialised than that of Adam Jukes, but, still, Watt has encountered several instances of male depression in the postnatal period. These patients did not come to him because of a new baby; instead, they were long-standing patients who became fathers while in analysis, experienced depressive episodes following the births of their children, and were able to work on their depression in their sessions with Watt. Watt also works in victim support for Southwark Council, mainly in the field of serious youth violence and gang lifestyles, supporting families and individuals in crisis.

Watt has seen many depressed fathers who have felt that their baby was replacing them; taking their place in the relationship with their partner, and taking their place in her affections. A new baby certainly does take over its mother, emotionally and physically – they both benefit from close physical contact in the first few months, and a mother will go through a certain amount of physical recovery and emotional adjustment – so it is easy to see how a father can become somewhat sidelined once the baby comes home. A father's role is less clearly defined, and so there is a sense that they are superfluous. The baby would still thrive without him around, and so this feeling of exclusion could contribute to depression. It is difficult for some fathers to cope with not knowing where they fit in, and the feeling of being excluded and the unhappiness that can stem from that is how postnatal depression often presents in Watt's male patients.

Exclusion can be experienced by fathers in many ways. Interestingly, Watt has worked with several men for whom religion has been the source of their exclusion. In these cases, up until the impending parenthood, the mother has been a certain religion, the father has not practised any religion; they are both accepting of this and there hasn't been an issue between them. The men have gone into the pregnancy thinking that the mother's religion plays a very minor role in the child's life – more a question of culture and heritage rather than ritual and practice – but, once the baby has arrived, the mother's feelings change and her religion is more important than ever. For the father involved, this creates even more of a bond between the mother and child, reinforcing his exclusion from their special relationship, leaving him feeling more superfluous and unnecessary than ever. In Watt's experience, this can particularly be the case in Judaism, and other matrilineal religions (where the religion is only passed down from mother to child), but of course things such as christening and baptism could also cause one parent to feel left out if the other has stronger religious beliefs.

Sometimes, the connection between the baby and mother can become a problem for the father in other ways. In some cases, the mother is closer to her extended family than the father is to his, and so they will end up seeing her 'side' more than his. Of course there are many reasons why one side is closer to the couple, but whatever they may be, they add to the feeling of there being a stronger connection between the mother and child.

Often, these feelings of exclusion will surface after the birth if they have been dormant in a man for some time. Sometimes men struggle to feel close to anyone – friends, family, and in particular their partner, and so the way their partner is suddenly so close to someone else and not them, compounds their existing feelings of exclusion. Of course, going from a partnership to a family of three is a huge change for a couple and maybe in particular for fathers. Before the baby arrived, the father had a connection with his partner, but after the birth he has no immediate connection with either his partner or his child. Instead, *she* has the direct connection with the child and the father is on the outside.

Watt makes an interesting observation about fathers and their resemblance to their children. We see it all the time – with jokes about a child being the 'milkman's' baby if it doesn't look particularly like the father; something as simple as an innocent (or not so innocent) joke about paternity that implies a closer connection between mother and child rather than father and child. When a woman is pregnant we can be fairly sure that she is the mother of the child (ren) she is carrying; there are more likely to be questions about paternity, should there be any questions at all. This is of course an anxiety that few men would actually face but certainly one (of maternity) that no woman would ever likely face.

There is an underlying question – what does it mean to be a man? And is this important to fathers? Of course, it is the fundamental concept of fatherhood – in order for the child to have been created there must also have been a man. For a father, though, their own masculinity and 'maleness' is always in question, because it becomes, on a conscious or subconscious level, crucially important to know that they are *the* father. It is also of crucial importance to know that they are *a* father – all sorts of questions are thrown up regarding what it means to be a father and whether they are being one or not. New fathers face these questions as soon as their partner becomes pregnant, and it can lead to concerns about their connection to their child in relation to the mother's connection.

Concerns about parental connections to the child often run deep. Without some self-awareness most men would not be aware of their own feelings surrounding this after the birth, or they might have difficulty identifying the cause of their changed behaviour and emotions. Anger, as we have already seen, is often a way that men show depression, whether it be directed at their partner, the baby, colleagues, or themselves. Watt agrees that anger is a facet of depression, and that anger or other behaviour is often masking a deep sense of sadness and loss. A father might experience feelings of loss because he feels he has lost out on the close connection the baby has with his partner, its mother, and so feels angry instead.

Watt tells me about a patient who, once his baby was born, threw himself into work and anything that involved being away from family life after becoming angry and unreasonable at home. He didn't want to spend any time there, and his partner probably didn't want him to either as a consequence. During psychoanalysis, it became clear that the man's behaviour stemmed from a feeling of not being attached to his child; of feeling emotionally cold and distant. Instead of taking steps to change this, the man had taken himself away from his wife and child, thus preventing the development of a bond with his child that deep down he really wanted. He feared that the child was never going to have the same relationship or connection that it had with its mother. The angry and distant behaviour confirmed what he already believed about the situation: that he was excluded. Watt notes that men often bring this behaviour and attitude to parenting

– that of the lone ranger, battling on their own to be a father, since they are always excluded from the special relationship between a mother and her child.

The huge, life-changing event of becoming a father also brings up another important emotion for men – that of envy. Women are the only ones who can grow, nourish and give birth to a baby. Certainly they need a man (or at least his sperm) in order to conceive the child, but, obviously, the male plays no part in childbearing. This feeling (of the mother doing something that the father cannot) only compounds the feelings of exclusion some men feel after they have a baby, and even before, as they watch their partner carry the child until the birth. They are completely excluded from her experience and can only look on and try to understand it as best they can – but this reinforces the strong connection they see between the mother and child and adds to the father's feelings of exclusion, which, again, can, occasionally, exacerbate feelings of depression in new fathers.

There is perhaps still a notion of man "sorting everything out" for their woman, being the main breadwinner, being stronger physically and emotionally, etc. Even if this is not the case, and many women would argue that it is not, it is still a prevalent view within our society, and this sense of men being 'masters of the universe' lingers on despite many changes in attitude and society. So, for men who feel as if they need to be masters of everything, anything they lack is a reflection on their potency – in extreme situations their wholeness and even their masculinity is called into question by being unable to bear children – an exclusively female part of life.

Watt has seen that a feeling of loss when a baby arrives is always a secondary elaboration of a loss previously felt. In order to deal with this, Watt says, the man must realise his previous loss and deal with its lack in the present. It is this acceptance of lack and loss which, according to Barry, is an integral part of being a man.

A father may feel envy, if only subconsciously, when his partner breastfeeds – again, this is a thing only women can do. The child has this close bond with its mother, who can provide nourishment and comfort with her body, and again, this leads back to a feeling of exclusion for the father. Often, negative feelings about breastfeeding are linked to early feelings in the father's life, when they had to eventually separate from their own mother and found it very difficult.

Breastfeeding can bring about negative emotions even if it doesn't go to plan. Watt tells me about one patient whose wife had difficulty breastfeeding and so the child was bottle fed. Instead of being glad of the opportunity for more involvement in the child's care, the father saw this as a failing of the mother. He felt that she was not being a good enough mother and not fulfilling her role. It is interesting to note that Watt puts his reaction down to envy; he was envious of the connection she had with their child *despite* not being able to breastfeed, and so this stirred up feelings of anger and resentment, all stemming from the way the child was to be fed.

According to Freud, all people, men and women, always go back to their early feelings and relationships and their future behaviour in relationships will be dictated and influenced by these early relationships in their lives. Every man therefore, according to Freud, is looking to replace his own mother – and so when the baby comes along and takes his 'mother' (his partner), it takes his place. When a mother has a child, and when it is an infant, it is as if they are one person. Early on there is a separation, where a child will realise it is a different person to its mother, and there will never be that same closeness and completeness ever again for a man. For a woman who has a child, that completeness can be briefly recaptured after the birth, but men will never experience this again, and so they can become envious of the fact that their partner *can* have this.

Anger, as we have seen with some of Adam Jukes' patients, can often lead to abuse in relationships. Sometimes this can be physical abuse, usually when the man is less emotionally secure and less emotionally intelligent. Sometimes it can be emotional abuse, with aggression driving constant put downs, slights, accusations that the mother is not doing her job properly, etc. Unfortunately, this sort of abuse is very common, but it is difficult to break free from, and difficult for a man to recognise his behaviour as abusive.

Many men who become abusive because of their depression surrounding childbirth rationalise their behaviour as an appropriate response to being put in second place. Of course, it is the baby who has 'put them in second place', and it is their partner who doesn't work hard enough to return them to their rightful position in her affections. They see their abuse as a legitimate expression of their own anger, but without realising why they are angry, or even that they are. There are some men who want the mother's experience, but they are often unable to make the imaginative leap that would enable them to understand it a bit better. And so instead of trying to understand their wife's position and accept it, they act out and get angry, and release their anger in the most inappropriate and unacceptable ways on their own families.

Some of the anger and difficulty men face surrounding childbirth is down to the 'crisis of masculinity' which is alive in our society at the present time. There has been a huge redefinition of gender roles during the last half a century and women have gone, very generally speaking, from housewives to breadwinners. The rise of equality in the workplace has seen women and men doing the same jobs and women having careers. There has also been an increased expectation for equality at home, so women now often are not left to do all the childcare and all the housework – men are expected to get involved in the domestic drudgery and to offer support with sleepless nights and crying babies once they become fathers.

However, this redefinition has happened very quickly, and despite this 'redefinition' there are no clearly defined roles, which adds to the feeling of that men have of not knowing their place once the baby arrives. This can, again, lead to them feeling excluded, since they know they are expected to be involved with the new baby, but they can't find a way to do so, their only model for the connection between parent and baby being the connection between the baby and its mother. The father can't have this connection and so feels excluded, and perhaps feels lost – what should he be doing? And why can't he have the same bond as his partner, when everyone says he should be a 'hands on' Dad?

Modern life can be a struggle for a man, particularly for a new father. Even though it is plausible that men do feel this envy over the connection the baby has with its mother, getting a father to admit that he is envious of his partner might be difficult. Men find it difficult to admit to having an envy of women – it would involve admitting to this 'lack' they have in their lives, and, because everything rests upon early childhood feelings and experiences, this would be phenomenally hard for a father to admit to. Women and men both form their views based on the discourse that is dominant in our society – for ours this is patriarchal. And we do live in a patriarchal society – one only has to look at the way childcare and maternity leave is arranged, and the importance placed on female attractiveness to see this. Despite this, the gender-based expectations men and women have of each other are not black and white – gender roles are not clearly defined or fixed, and there will be countless familial situations where typically male and female roles will be blurred.

However with the current blurred roles, there is a traditional role that has somewhat stuck; the father is the 'law' in a family unit. Children are told "go and ask your father", which, as a consequence, has the last word – the buck stops with Dad. But the father, according to Watt, in his law-giving, has to represent his partner's views also, his laws have to reflect the laws of everyone. He has to be the one to rule his family and to be part of the ruling gender of the world. but he is doomed to fail at this, and fathers wrestle with this impossible role that is thrust upon them by society. This is a view very much linked to the traditional role of the man in within the family and in society, and perhaps it is less relevant now – although these traditional concepts are difficult for society to shake off. Often, as we have already seen, fathers can become distant figures in the parental couple. This could be a reaction to the depression they feel having been given this impossible role to fulfil – the father cannot cope with what is expected of him, and so he takes himself away from the family unit so he doesn't have to face it. They make themselves absent, often by legitimate means like throwing themselves into work and putting in long hours, or sometimes by going out drinking, playing golf, or chasing other women. However they do it, perhaps this is the reason why – they can't deal with themselves as fathers. Watt points out that a man, particularly a father, has to learn to tolerate this split position of being in a role which is impossible to fulfil. Finding a way to negotiate this impossibility and still remain in the role as a present father is very difficult for some men, but until the expectations of fathers change, there is not much which can be done.

The discourse surrounding gender clearly needs work, and perhaps it will take many years for it to settle into something more concrete and easy to live with for both sexes. However, the discourse about postnatal depression might be a good place to start so that men can be acknowledged. The inclusion of men in the way PND is talked about may cause anger with some groups of women, and men. It should be framed with caution, says Watt, and not in a way that overshadows the suffering of women.

Things like male-focused antenatal classes will help men to negotiate their way through this landscape. Issues that men face need to be part of everyday discourse, and emotions such as anger, envy and exclusion should be addressed before a man becomes a father. Fathers perhaps need to share their experiences more and more with each other so that these feelings don't appear without warning. Women should also be made aware so that they can recognise and deal with their partner's behaviour.

In the Western world, it is increasingly impossible for a man to be the traditional man – they are having to give it up in favour of something else; some other view of masculinity and manhood is taking its place. But many men will see this as 'feminising' themselves, which, although it isn't making them feminine, the idea alone would be enough to make it difficult for many men to achieve.

Watt says that depression is really just anger turned inwards. He talks about a patient who was very keen to be the 'nice guy' and made every effort to be polite, conscientious, and a good person to be around – at work, out with friends, and at home with his family. He had a lot of anger, but worked very hard to curtail it in order to maintain his 'nice guy' status. In order to achieve this the anger had to go somewhere and so it was turned upon himself, which made him very depressed.

Perhaps men who become depressed after the birth of their child are really just redirecting the anger they feel, because of this difficult situation they find themselves in, back on themselves. It is certainly something to be aware of, especially in cases where the man has suffered from depression before the birth but seems fine afterwards – there may still be unresolved anger issues.

But perhaps these discussions with psychoanalysts are not helpful in the discussion of paternal postnatal depression, since what we have heard from both Adam Jukes and Barry Watt is that they haven't seen any men come to them specifically with the problem that they are depressed after becoming a father, or if this has been an issue, such men have been fortunate enough to already be involved in therapy to deal with the problems as and when they cropped up. In many cases, men have come to seek help only when their lives have unravelled so much that they can't pinpoint where it all started to go wrong. There is no doubt that analysis and therapy can help men suffering from postnatal depression, but it is clear – if Watts' and Jukes' experiences represent the situation in general – that there is always going to be a huge difficulty in getting men with PPND to seek help.

CHAPTER FIVE

Men as dependent on women

Men can get angry when they get depressed. Men can be envious of their partners, and they can feel pushed out of their relationship by their own child. But why do men feel this way? Susie Orbach and Luise Eichenbaum in their book *What Do Women Want?* (originally published in 1983) have some interesting answers to this question, with a fascinating discussion of men's dependency on women. I would like to focus on that here, as well as the implications for the couple and their dependency dynamic once the baby is born.

As I have already discussed, men are commonly seen as the providers in the family. It is often their responsibility to be the breadwinner, and to protect the family, remaining strong and unemotional so that the family can lean on them. Men are expected to hide any hint of weakness and must not appear vulnerable, since they are supposed to be the ones holding everyone else up. If they do show vulnerability, the traditional view of masculinity is shattered, and they become fearful, insecure, and in need of comfort and reassurance.

Orbach says that women are attracted to both the strong and vulnerable sides of men's personalities. It is true that most women only describe falling in love with a man when he exposes his more vulnerable 'feminine' side – when he allows them to see this "hidden" side of him. However close we get to equality, there remains a sense of it being a man's world, and a world in which women need a man to make them feel safe and looked after. It is very difficult to shed these traditional ideas. Men are aware of what is expected of them with regards to masculinity too; aware that they need to act like 'men' in order to woo a woman since this is what women are supposed to be attracted to. At the same time, a man wants to find someone to share his vulnerable side with, but this is usually a partner: not all men share their emotional side with other men.

The way masculinity (and femininity) influences how men and women act in relationships is evidence of how we are all at the mercy of a patriarchal culture. Because of this, men might feel that they are not allowed to freely express their emotions, since they are expected by society to grow up and be a 'man' – that is grow up and have the power to act in the world. But in order to become a man in this patriarchal society a boy must disassociate from the world of his mother and identify with his father. This is a significant event for a boy, since his mother's world is his first world and all he has known, but he must leave that world, the world of women and join the unfamiliar and strange world of his father. What makes it so difficult for the young boy is that he has taken into his own personality aspects of his mother's personality, because he has been so close to her during the first year of his life. As a little boy grows, he sees that he is separate from his mother and is different from her – he begins to identify more with his father because of their shared gender.

Gender awareness occurs from around the age of 2, when a boy learns that he is not like his mother. Not in all cases, but certainly in many families, and regardless of their best efforts to keep toys neutral, a boy learns that he must not play with girl's toys, must keep femininity out, and must play at 'going out to work' and with guns and tools. As time goes on this identification with maleness and masculinity solidifies and the boy wants to be like Daddy, but in order to do this he must deny all the ways he is like Mummy. A boy is encouraged to win and succeed and to compete with other boys – these are all aspects of masculinity dictated by our patriarchal society. Mummy is still there of course, but her role is to provide her son with love and support, but she too contributes to this perception of masculinity, and her actions, as well as the child's father's, will support and perpetuate society's view of what men and boys *should* be like. A mother giving birth to a son is aware of the way her son will be treated by society, and knows that it is different from her experience purely because of her gender. A mother will encourage her son to 'be a man,' and in doing so will play a part in her son's disassociation from her.

According to Orbach, men are split. There are two parts to their psychology – one part acts in accepted 'masculine' ways, and is seen by the world; the other part is representative of their deep connection to their mothers as infants, and is buried deep in the unconscious. It is important to note, however, that even though this aspect of their personality is hidden, boys will still rely on their mothers for support and care. Mothers, of course, encourage and nurture their sons (and their daughters too), by caring for them, feeding them, and clothing them. A boy can look forward to this sort of care later in life from his partner, who will mostly replace his mother in this role. Crucially, this is not the case for girls, who grow up and perhaps don't depend on their partners in the same way, and so their dependency needs are not met. This sort of conflict, or split, in a man's psychology can cause problems in relationships (both romantic and otherwise) as an adult, and, as we have seen, can cause problems when a new baby enters the relationship.

It is common for a woman who is a mother to still go out to work, but this often has little effect on the division of labour at home, and so a man will continue to have all his domestic needs met by his partner – they continue to have a 'mother'. Again, this is not the case for women – they do not have a mother looking after them at home, they are that mother. Some households, of course, are much more equal. A man might do his own ironing, and share the everyday tasks such as laundry, cooking and cleaning equally with his partner. However, his partner can continue to be a mother to him and to fulfil his need for dependency by being there emotionally and providing the encouragement that a man might have received from his mother as a boy. In this way there is often a seamless continuation of the dependency experience, at the same time as they are out in the world making money and gaining power.

Furthermore, 'women's work' – all the traditional duties of being a mother and a housewife – has been invisible and unrecognised in society until quite recently (and arguably is still unrecognised by many). Take, for instance, the way in which women are usually expected to be the hostess and to make guests feel at ease, or the way women are often expected to maintain good relations with the wider family – these situations highlight aspects of how men are dependent on women, while ultimately being oblivious to it as it's accepted as being completely normal by society. Some mothers are still finding it difficult to acknowledge their role as being hard work, and there are those who feel that mothers who don't work 'do nothing all day' without any real regard for how much work is involved. At the same time, some men have not acknowledged their own vulnerable side and or their continuing dependency on women. Because we live in a patriarchal society it can be difficult to accept these truths, which remind people of how powerful women actually are.

As I already mentioned, all babies must at some point, separate from their mothers in order to become little boys and girls and to form their own identity in the world. However, for boys, their ability to separate means that they have to cultivate their own set of defences so that they can develop a sense of themselves as male. (This happens for girls too, but our focus is on boys and men here.) Having these defences means that they have to strike a fine balance between keeping a healthy sense of themselves as independent beings, and an unhealthy distancing of themselves and other people, so as to keep people away and make sure they don't get too close – so, according to Orbach, that they don't discover the side of a man or boy which is like his mother; sensitive, vulnerable and emotional.

Our patriarchal society does not prepare boys for their role as a father, particularly in terms of what is expected of fathers nowadays – boys simply aren't raised in a way which enables them to make this transition easily. Now fathers are expected to be involved in their baby's care, and to get involved in childcare and birth, but their upbringing as a boy does little to prepare them for this. It is still the case that girls are encouraged, by the media or by their parents and peers, to play with dolls and tea sets, and are often told to 'be nice' (meaning they shouldn't fight, and should be selfless). While this early stereotyping into gender roles is oppressive to women, it could be said that it does at least prepare them for motherhood since they are given the opportunity to develop their own potential for nurturing and caring for other people.

Boys, however, are not encouraged to play in the same ways. They are encouraged to play with cars, guns, and tools, and can be ridiculed for playing with what are considered 'girls' toys' – they are never allowed to identify with their mother and with femininity. From the start, then, we (the media, parents, and peers) make it difficult for some boys to develop nurturing characteristics, and any aspects of themselves that are like their mothers are forced to remain hidden away, not acceptable to society. These ideas of girls and boys are deep-rooted. In this patriarchal society it is incredibly difficult for us to change the way children are treated, despite our best efforts to keep toys and attitudes gender neutral. Perhaps we are setting up our sons to fail at fatherhood, or at the very least, we are leaving some of them vulnerable to difficulties and depression when they do become fathers.

When men become fathers what does this mean for their dependency on women? And why do children have such an effect? Orbach devotes an entire chapter to this issue in her book, and again, I will refer mainly to what she has to say. Dependency is an issue at the forefront of every expectant parent's mind – that is, the dependency of the baby. The infant will need their care and attention, and will be vulnerable and dependent upon its parents to stay alive. Typically, mothers and fathers have different reactions to the realisation that their infant will be wholly dependent upon them, with a woman being worried about whether she is able to give enough love to the child, and the man more likely to worry about providing for his family. Even before the baby is here we can see differences in how the arrival is anticipated, and this is, again, due to the society in which we live. Although in creating the child the couple should have been joint decision makers, everything else is unbalanced. Even if the couple go into parenthood with the idea that parenting is a mutual and shared experience they will be surprised when they realise that this is not the case.

Orbach points out the understanding of the intimacy between a mother and child and a father and child will underpin this realisation, bolstered by the expectations that women will be the primary caretakers. As I have said before, although women go out to work just as much as men do, once they become mothers they are likely to be the ones more closely connected to the child; more intimate with them, and they will be the first port of call for all their child's needs. Mothers spend the most time with their infant in the immediate postnatal period, and so become attuned to their needs. What often happens is that by an infant becoming dependent on his or her mother, a mother in return becomes more emotionally close to her children than to her partner. This can make a father feel more like an outsider than he already does (because of the close, physical relationship a mother has with her child). If a father is out at work all day they are *physically* 'not there'; he can then become *emotionally* 'not there' when he gets home, because his partner is seemingly getting all her emotional fulfilment from their child instead of him.

The dependency of the infant often causes changes in the way dependency functioned between the couple before the baby arrived. These changes can happen while a woman is pregnant, since pregnant women often feel vulnerable carrying a new life inside them, and as a consequence they lean on their partner more than before. Some men find this difficult, and cannot cope well with having their partner so dependent on them, especially since this was the person they were so dependent upon in the first place. A man might feel like he has to rebel, and as a consequence stays away from the home in an attempt to make their partners able to manage without them again, and to regain some of the balance that was there in their relationship before the pregnancy. As we have seen in previous chapters, men affected by peri- or postnatal depression often have affairs outside of their relationships. Sexual affairs while their partner is pregnant or has just become a mother are surprisingly common – it is when sex can be scarce, haphazard, or even non-existent. As I have discussed, fathers can feel forgotten while their baby is so small because the mother is entirely focused on their child. – she does most of the parenting and has to give most of her attention to her infant.

Orbach says that this can remind a father of the time when he was a young boy and realised that his mother was not his – she had another man – his father, and he became aware of the importance of their relationship, which did not involve him. Now as a father himself, he feels the same sense of being replaced by another person who takes away his 'mother's' attention. His dependency on his partner is unfulfilled, and so the father finds a temporary replacement for his partner by having an affair.

But at the same time as feeling pushed away by their partners, men too push them away by having an affair. Men can be very bad at managing their own dependency needs and don't see this shift in dependency as a temporary or necessary thing, and so because they are so scared of being abandoned by their partners they look elsewhere for someone to give them what they need. Affairs can, of course, have a long-lasting effect on a couple's relationship, which, of course, as mentioned, has an effect on a child's development. For instance, when an affair is uncovered, even if the couple decide to stay together, the relationship and its dynamics can be changed forever. There can be trust issues, a man's fear of intimacy and of showing his vulnerable side can come to the forefront again, meaning that the couple cannot be as close as they were before. A woman would feel less secure in the relationship. – all these things would affect the couple's behaviour, and as a consequence might have an affect on the child. And, all these feelings are a result of a man's dependency needs being unfulfilled due to a new baby, which, as we have seen, is something men young and old are woefully underprepared for.

Similarly, men can, and do, have affairs while their wives are pregnant. Many women feel an increased desire for sex during pregnancy, and so for men the excuse of having an affair because his partner is not interested in sex is perhaps often untrue. As well as when the baby has been born, pregnancy can also be a time when men feel excluded, as they may feel jealous of the relationship their wife already has with the baby – an intimate relationship with someone apart from with them. Again, this can awaken old experiences of these fathers losing their mothers' attention while they were little boys; of realising that they were not the only important person in their mother's life. Again, the dependency dynamic in the couple is shifted, and some men cannot cope with it.

Other than having affairs, men who are depressed postnatally can display other types of behaviour which would indicate that they cannot deal with the change in the dependency dynamic in their relationships after a baby is born. For example, some men start spending more and more time at work, or anywhere, *other* than being at home with his partner and child. Orbach works through an example of this in her book. A woman can become more dependent on her partner while she is pregnant, we have already discussed this above. Women may want more emotional support, the most independent of women might feel like they need their partner to attend their medical appointments with them, and to spend more time with them and do more things for them. As a consequence, men have to be more emotionally involved with their partners than they are used to, and they have to accept that their partner is more dependent on them at this time. Men can feel resentful at this – their own upbringing has not prepared them for this part of their lives, and they can feel like too much is being asked of them. They don't know *how* to have someone depend upon them in this emotional way, since they are used to the roles being reversed.

The fact that there is not outside recognition for their emotional support of their partner is also difficult for some men – no one is going to see them caring for their wife and fulfilling their partner's dependency needs. It is certainly not very 'manly', and not what they would have played at with other little boys when they were small. So by going out to work a man feels like he is actually *doing* something. People would recognise that he is achieving things, he gets paid, possibly promoted, and he is providing for his family – all the things which fit in much better with him being a man.

For some couples, pregnancy and afterwards is a time when they become closer and their relationship becomes stronger. Some couples allow themselves to be taken over by the commitment, the attachment, and the dependency, and as a consequence they feel more secure and more settled as their years of family life begin. A couple who were previously preoccupied with work, and perhaps leading separate lives, are now given a new focus and brought together with the arrival of a baby, which gives them a shared project, something which links them together and makes them stronger. It is an opportunity for men and women to open themselves up and allow them to have an intimate relationship with a new person.

CHAPTER SIX

The dangers of childbirth for men – A discussion with Michel Odent

The first person to contribute to this book was Michel Odent; in fact, the book was inspired by his ideas, since paternal post-partum depression is a subject that is not unfamiliar to him. He wrote a chapter entitled 'Male postpartum depression' for a book *Perinatal Mental Health: A Clinical Guide* (2012) because he believed, and still believes, that it is vital that health-care professionals are aware of this condition. Odent himself is a renowned obstetrician; he directed the surgical and maternity unit at Pithiviers Hospital in France (1962–1985) where he developed his interest in the birth process. After that he founded the Primal Health Research Centre in London and also became involved in home birth. More recently he has trained 'doulas', who are women operating somewhere between the role of a midwife and a trusted friend. They are non-medical, but are there to assist a woman (and her partner) before, during and after childbirth, providing physical and emotional support. Now in his eighties, Odent continues to work internationally, giving lectures and writing papers. He is also the author of several books on all aspects of birth.

Odent is the only person I have talked to with a medical background – a phenomenon like paternal post-partum depression is more likely to be acknowledged amongst those involved in mental health, such as psychotherapists, counsellors, etc. His first-hand experience of many births has given him a vast bank of knowledge about the behaviour of fathers during and after a birth, although he admits that it is only since becoming more involved in home birth that he has become aware of how a father is affected – as a hospital practitioner he didn't think of the new father at all. It is easy to comprehend that a father might be feeling fragile or vulnerable having witnessed a birth, but Odent claims they can be physically fragile as well. His view of post-partum depression in fathers is that it is almost never seen in fathers who haven't attended the birth of their child – he is very clear that there is a link between symptoms and attendance. Now that birth is an event that calls for a father to be present (in this country and many Western nations), this is an important correlation, since the question must be asked – has such a change contributed to poor paternal mental health?

Shockingly, Odent told me two separate stories of paternal post-partum death. The idea of any parent dying after the birth of their child is devastatingly sad, and Odent is convinced that there *is* a link, in these cases, between the birth and the apparently unrelated death of these fathers.

The first story concerns a Russian couple from Moscow. Odent describes them as 'New Age' people – their dream was to have the baby in the Indian Ocean, and they travelled there with this intention. Odent met up with the mother, who was the second wife of her older husband Alexis, in Moscow after the birth. She told him how beautiful the whole experience had been, so much so that she had decided to write about it in her book, which Odent showed me while I sat with him.

The book is in Russian, but the text was unimportant, since what Odent wanted to show me were the pictures. Alexis, the father, is always 'highly visible' in the photographs, which shows just how involved he was in the whole process had been tasked with finding and choosing an exact location for the birth to take place, an important task since he would be the one helping his wife. The baby was born in the sea as planned with Alexis playing the role of midwife – such hands on help is really above and beyond what is expected of today's modern fathers. Odent, not wanting to pry, and perhaps sensing what was coming, didn't ask the new mother about Alexis but spoke to some mutual friends instead. Devastatingly, following the birth, Alexis had died suddenly after a heart attack while still in India.

Of course, remarks Odent, the man probably had coronary heart disease, undiagnosed and lying in wait, but Odent found timing of the death very interesting. Men are fragile, says Odent, and they are particularly fragile after witnessing and participating in their child's birth. Alexis was there with his wife and supporting her and their baby during its journey into the world – could this experience really have triggered his death?

The second story Odent came across on the internet, but it caught his attention so he made further enquiries to find out more. A father had slipped into a coma and died after holding his newborn son for the first and only time. The man had a heart condition and had undergone some sort of operation to do with this before the birth – he was ill, but he managed to live until just after his baby was born. This sort of story is the type of thing we sometimes see in magazines, the focus being that the father, wonderfully, at least got to meet his baby son and hold him before he died. This undeniably sad event was devastating for the parents and families involved, so perhaps no link would ever have been made between the father being present at the birth and his subsequent death.

Clearly, these are upsetting links to be making, and since they are based only on anecdotal evidence, and there is no scientific basis to them at all. There is no way of knowing in advance whether a man will be significantly affected by being in attendance at the birth, and virtually no way of knowing *when* someone afflicted by an known or unknown life-threatening condition is going to die.

The second story centres around The Whittington Hospital in North London, whose newsletter Odent once saw praising the value of the medical team who had two separate opportunities to impress a couple with their medical expertise. A couple had been in the hospital for the birth of their first child, a big baby, who was to be induced due to its size. The baby had become distressed during the birth, and the medical team had had to act quickly to perform an emergency caesarean section to deliver the baby safely. Some days later the father came to the hospital to collect his partner and their baby but unexpectedly collapsed in the corridor. The same team who had delivered the baby had had to resuscitate the man, and had subsequently saved his life. The two events seem unrelated – but for Odent the timing is, once again, significant. Even if an unknown medical condition had affected the man who collapsed, the fact he had been present at the birth of his child some days earlier had, perhaps, had an impact.

During the months I spent researching this book I came across a story like Odent's – where a father had been taken ill immediately after the birth of his child. In this case, the father had a known, pre-existing autoimmune condition that had been mostly under control for many years, apart from the occasional flare up. His wife had a difficult pregnancy, and was admitted to hospital on several occasions during the last trimester with non-life- threatening, but serious and uncomfortable, complications. On top of this, the couple had three children to care for. Before the birth, the father was complaining of feeling unwell, but then his wife went into labour, slightly before her due date, and he attended the birth, as he had done for the arrival of his other children. A week or so after the birth, once mother and baby were home again, the father collapsed and was admitted to hospital – his autoimmune condition requiring urgent treatment and medication. He came out of hospital after a short stay, but was unable to participate in the care for the new baby; he felt dizzy much of the time, was unwilling to hold the baby because he felt so feverish and uncomfortable, and spent a lot of time recovering in bed while his wife was left to care for him and their four children. Speaking to the wife and mother after the situation was back to normal and her husband had returned to work full-time, she was certain that the stress surrounding the birth had triggered his illness; she had wondered whether he'd had postnatal depression and admitted it was hard to see that this could have happened as a result of his long-standing condition. .

During the nineties, Odent organised and ran information sessions for doulas. They would often tell him about mysterious ailments the men had complained of after their partners had given birth, and so he asked them to look at the behaviour of fathers during and after the birth experience and report back. He was subsequently presented with a huge range of physical afflictions, such as knee pain, kidney stones, appendicitis, rashes, abscesses – the onset sudden and without a known cause. The men therefore required dermatologists, physiotherapists, and physicians, who, as expected, perhaps, made no enquiry about their recent experience. As a consequence, says Odent, such symptoms that present themselves after the birth are almost always put down to bad luck, coincidence, or a pre-existing condition.

Traditionally, labour is 'women's business.' Women laboured among other women, and gave birth among other women, and a man was presented with the fruit of their loins once everything had been cleaned away and their wife was, once again, looking radiant. This is obviously a far cry from what happens now, and birth has also become much more medicalised – until the early 1900s it didn't take place in a hospital at all. A rough guess is that 90% of fathers are with their partners when they go through labour. There from the very beginning, they often stay with their partner for hours, even days, right up until the moment of birth, which they witness. Sometimes they even get involved by cutting the umbilical cord, or just help their partner with their breathing, and offer words of encouragement. Perhaps because of all this, men are aware of the physiological details of birth, can understand contractions, dilation etc, all so that they can be a support for their partner – but where is their support? And do they need it?

For Odent, the father's presence at a birth has raised important questions but there is no one to address them. There is a fundamental cultural misunderstanding, says Odent, about birth not being a natural process. This means that humans have found ways to interfere with the process of birth for thousands of years, whether it is by the introduction of a midwife or other female figure, or, more recently, a doctor and anaesthetist. Although by name 'natural childbirth' claims to restore childbirth to how it should be, it did little to address this misunderstanding. Odent talks about the Lamaze method as an example. This method of birth preparation bases its strategy on reconditioning the natural behaviour of a labouring woman, and an active role was given to birth attendants, but really, says Odent, this stimulates a part of a woman's brain, the neocortex, responsible for sensory perception, conscious thought, and language – all the things a labouring woman does not need when she is giving birth. According to Odent, there is a 'foetal expulsion reflex' that occurs in a woman's body that enables the baby to be born without any voluntary pushing on her part, but this never happens if the woman is too crowded by people, let alone if the father is there. He refers to a Persian proverb, which reads 'when there are two midwives the baby's head is crooked,' similar to the well-known saying 'too many cooks spoil the broth.' Of course, there are many situations where medical intervention and observation is necessary for the survival of both the mother and the baby, and in no way is Odent suggesting that women give birth without the correct medical care, is it just interesting to look at the potential benefits of minimal intervention in labour.

Really, this illustrates not only how misunderstood birth is, and how different it is now from how it *should* be, but also show how little understanding there is for a mother during the process. Fathers, or other birth partners, are seen as assisting a woman in labour, but no thought is given to whether they actually need to be there or how it might affect them , and the effects, as we have seen, can be both physical and emotional; it can be risky for some men to be at the birth of their child. This will impact upon mothers too, since many women do need the support of their partner after childbirth, but if a man is expected to watch and be involved in childbirth and he is tipped over the edge into anxiety and avoidance behaviours at the very thought of it, then he is of no use to the new mother and will probably be impacting negatively on their relationship. Isn't it best all round to understand that some men *need* to be absent from birth?

One recurring theme Odent has seen regarding men's mental health is, again, this need to escape from their new reality, and he has his own examples of this type of behaviour. He told me about the author of a book about childbirth whose husband had developed an 'irresistible need' to play golf following the birth of their baby. Other things must have happened in between, but the couple divorced and she cites his golf obsession as the trigger for the collapse of the marriage. Odent sees this sort of behaviour as self-protection – the father was desperate to escape his new situation, and so instead of sticking around and being ill, he escaped. Whether this was a conscious decision it is not clear. Maybe he presented it to his wife as needing to play golf in order to entertain business contacts, or to get more exercise, or some other excuse, but for Odent the golf was an excuse to get away from the baby and his new role as a father.

There are many incidences Odent has come across similar to this one. He had an acquaintance that was a neonatologist, and so was familiar with births in hospitals. His wife, however, decided to give birth at home and so we can assume he was involved in, and present at, the birth, and yet for days afterwards he could not stop playing computer games. Again, he needed to escape. In this case, the problem didn't last, and as far as Odent knows this didn't trigger any relationship problems, but it is interesting to note how, in most cases, this would be seen as unnecessary behaviour, and the man being deliberately unsupportive and not pulling their weight, rather than the necessary behaviour of a fragile man trying to protect himself.

As I said at the start of the book, male depression is not as clear cut as female depression in that male depression is hidden behind a veil of symptoms – it is covert. This is not a new idea among mental health professionals, but the notion of post-partum depression in men is not something that is talked about. As mentioned, Odent did write about it for *Perinatal Mental Health: A Clinical Guide* (2012), which he believes was important, because so often psychologists are not aware. Odent himself has only ever come across one example of a man who actively saw a psychiatrist because of his mental health after the birth of his child. Again, it was a home birth, and so the father was present and perhaps more involved than he would have been in a hospital setting. He had suffered from panic attacks, but the psychiatrist apparently made no link between the birth and these attacks, and prescribed anti-depressants after making his diagnosis of covert depression. It may be that in this case (and others) a link is made between becoming a father and depression, since it is a huge, fundamental change to undergo, but I expect that there is almost never a link made between presence at a birth and subsequent mental health problems – this is what Odent seeks to change.

Marjorie Tew talks about the first 'birth attendants' in her book *Safer Childbirth?*(1998), where she notes that those called upon to help were probably the mother's female relations or friends, who would have learned their skill from watching births and from their own labours. Eventually these sorts of women went through formal training, and practised as midwifes in much the same way as we know today. She continues that the historic function of midwives was to give continuous companionship and support, as well as help physically with the birth. After births were hospitalised in the twentieth century, women had to fight for attendants or companions to be allowed back in, and this included fathers, who had been excluded and were often found waiting in the corridor outside. Hospitals and doctors saw the inclusion of companions, especially those who had been through antenatal classes, as beneficial, not least because it lessened their workload in an already overstretched environment.

Men were protected during childbirth because they were kept busy; in some cultures the father was given the task of boiling water – a task that could go on for hours and hours and that had no purpose except to give him something to do. It was a kind of ritual, and similar rituals were in place in other cultures around the world, simply to protect the father. A ritual could be a simple as going to the pub – perhaps less nowadays, but certainly in the past it wouldn't have been unheard of for a man to decamp to the local public house to seek the solace of some other male company and some beer. A father is full of adrenalin when his partner is in labour, and doulas have often reported to Odent that men can reach extreme emotional states at this time. Some have observed (at home births) men clenching their fists, or biting their tongues, and one has even reported a father urinating in his trousers during the birth. A ritual or a task to keep a man busy during this time can be essential to distract and to use that adrenalin so that the father doesn't feel so tense.

Men are, in general, used to hiding their emotional state, and so an experienced doula can recognise the importance of busying the new father. Odent tells me about one doula who witnessed a father meticulously preparing a room for the birth of his child, cleaning it and covering areas with protective sheeting. She knew that the labouring mother would not give birth in that room, but allowed him to continue with his task to keep him busy and away from the actual birth. Odent points out that a couple's relationship – their sex life or the man's sexual attraction to his partner – is often affected as a direct result of a man witnessing his child's birth. It is certainly a worry to some women that their partners will watch the baby emerge and then be turned off by them sexually, forever! Odent also points out that these theories about the many benefits of men's presence at birth are almost never expressed by the people directly involved in childbirth – the midwives – rather they are the product of 'studies' by people removed from frontline action – academics, sociologists, theorists, and the like.

Odent has attended many home births over the past ten years. Through his involvement with doulas he took a back seat and would often stay with the father in another room to keep his mind busy and his presence elsewhere. The doula would stay with the mother for the birth and only after the birth and the delivery of the placenta would the father be introduced to his newborn child. Invariably in these situations, says Odent, the father would be proud of his partner and filled with respect and love for her, and his attachment to his new baby would be based on this reinforced love for his partner. This attachment between father and baby was virtually unrecognised in the seventies – a time when attachment and bonding between a mother and a baby was key. Scientists had 'discovered' that a baby needs maternal love, and that there is a specific hormonal balance between a mother and baby that cannot be replicated. Theoreticians dreamed of a similar, intense bonding between a father and baby, which played a part in the introduction of new models of childbirth, involving both the mother and the father. However, Odent stresses again that these new childbirth situations leave many, complex questions unanswered.

Odent has written extensively about childbirth, but his views remain controversial – essentially he says we have changed how childbirth *should* be with the advent of modern medicine. Certainly women are built to give birth without medical intervention, but even if we acknowledge this, we cannot ignore the fact that modern medicine has saved lives

– and in terms of childbirth there are countless babies and mothers who would not be alive today without doctors (and midwives). There are two extremes to his argument. Odent's views on fathers attending the births of their children are no less controversial, and will perhaps be difficult for many to agree with, but it is worth acknowledging them. They might hold true for some men, which could save them (and consequently their families) unnecessary suffering. Even if they don't, it is interesting to include such a controversial standpoint in the discussion of paternal postnatal depression – there are no hard and fast answers and so we must explore every avenue.

CHAPTER SEVEN

The evolution of the father

What *is* a father? Fathers and mothers have existed for millennia. The human race drives forward; our need to survive keeps us reproducing, but fatherhood, and what fathers *do*, has changed immeasurably since our caveman days. But do our roots still affect what it means to be a parent? And what can this mean for postnatal depression? Has it always existed, in one form or another? Aldo Naouri, in his book *Fathers and Mothers* (2005), argues that in Western societies the father has lost his status as the central member of the family, and has been replaced by the child; this can damage the development of the child, since the father no longer has a central role. I shall not go too far into his argument about child development here, but I will discuss what he has to say about evolution and the new, diminished role of the father, and the possible implications of this on a father's mental state.

Family groups, as we know them today, are quite a late, evolutionary phenomenon. Humans travelled in large groups, in which there were subgroups, and later on sub-subgroups, and then couples started to establish themselves, which enabled the 'family' to be established too – a mother, father, and children. Mothers were, and are, central to childbearing and childrearing. They've held a central place from one end of the evolutionary chain to the other, and she alone grows the child within her – no-one else carries out this task for her.

The father, on the other hand, has always had a lesser part to play in childbearing. For thousands of years the only thing driving a man to reproduce was his sexual desire. Later, as the man became part of a couple, he would have started to establish his place as a social father, and in being linked to one female exclusively, it would have been known that her offspring were also his. The modern idea of a father is a very recent thing.

For Naouri, males started off not even knowing they were fathers, since all they cared about was satisfying their sexual desires; they were without direction until they fought with each other, thus learning to fear death. For females the awareness of death perhaps came through infant mortality and miscarriage. Naouri suggests that the two sexes never discussed death; however, this awareness would have meant that men wanted to find a way to get rid of the anxiety it brought them, and they did this by learning to take control over their animalistic, sexual impulses, which led to the formation of couples, the binding of male and female companions, and the slow formation of laws surrounding these small family groups.

Men formed families to ensure that they always had their female with them (and their offspring) and thus made sure that they held the top position. Their status as head of the family was engineered by them, and they ruled over their partners and children – this is the original 'father'. This process has left us with an imprint on the human psyche – the father is the law giver, he is also bound by those laws, and he has an interest in his offspring and partner. So, for Naouri, this longstanding notion of fatherhood is based on the universal awareness of time and the acceptance of the mortality of the human condition.

Naouri argues that fathers have been ejected from this central position in the family structure on account of being 'nebulous', in contrast to women who he describes as 'solid'. Despite being objects of sexual desire, and the thing that males have argued over, females have retained their capacity to be mothers and raise their offspring; they are 'solid' because this role has remained a constant. Fathers, on the other hand are 'nebulous': uncertain of who they are and of who they are supposed to be, they are vague and ill-defined. Mothers have always known they are mothers, but the creation of the father was a slow process. The wide variety of societies and cultures around the globe and the differences between the laws they prescribe illustrates the nebulosity of the father in much more recent times.

For instance, laws concerning ownership of children were in the father's favour in Roman and Arab-Islamic societies, and yet the notion that a father could have more claim to his children that their mother has always been contested, and laws like this have been adapted and changed, coming up against opposition, no doubt from mothers. This lack of uniformity and lack of acceptance of the rights of the father over those of the mother suggest that mothers and fathers are not equal. The solidity of the mother cannot be matched by a similar solidity of the father – mothers have always had control over children – and so the nebulosity of the father has in some ways been universally accepted, even though men will always try to gain some control, and reinstate their own position as head of the family, in charge of everyone and everything.

What about the physical differences between men and women? Can these too be described as 'solid' and 'nebulous'? If we look at the genitalia of men and women the concepts are reversed. Women's genitalia are discreet, and yet they enable a woman to become a solid mother. A man's genitals are obvious, more pronounced, and yet after he has impregnated a female he is left with no advantage in respect of parenthood – he is nebulous. A man cannot hide his sexuality, and if we look back to cave paintings he didn't want to – men are clearly depicted as men, and they used their physical appendage as part of their power over women. Yet he is also fully dependent on women because they have the power to satisfy him, physically, and such power has always been a burden to him. He cannot hide his need for women, or the satisfaction he gains from them, and so he is always both vulnerable and predictable. This sexual drive has ruled men for millennia, and men have tried to control and manage it by giving women strict rules so that they have control over their relationship with their children. The father sees the child as a threat to his sexual drive, and a threat to the couple.

Because the roles of 'father' and 'mother' have changed somewhat, this has had an effect on the concept of the 'nebulous' father – it is replaced by two opposing models that both differ greatly from the original concept: The first model is that of the 'vindictive' father who is keen to assert his rights and thinks he can take up a position of solidity like the mother. The second is the 'seductive' father, who tries to be like the mother and tries to compete with her, thus disappearing completely as a father without knowing that's what he's doing.

The vindictive father has always existed; an abuser who controls everything, including his partner who he makes powerless, either by physical or emotional means. This sort of father believes he is master of everything, and this causes great harm because their claim to solidity goes against maternal solidity, which he claims is established by his role as a biological father to his child. Naouri suggests that the first model of fatherhood is too closely linked to the unconscious mind of the primitive father, who was murdered by his sons, or feared that he would be, and took steps to make sure that didn't happen – he made sure he retained the power. Unfortunately many fathers like this still exist and give rise to situations where, for instance, they will battle for custody of their children, when it is clear that the children need to be with their mother.

The seductive father is a newer concept – we might call it the 'new father' – borne out of the social changes of the last fifty years, which have aimed to bring about equality. There was a need to invent a new kind of father; one which helped with domestic tasks and provided paternal help The father then became attentive and maternal, like the child's mother, and encouraged and bolstered the mother's fierce protection of her child. This has had a negative effect on the child, and also on the couple; this second father, according to Naouri, is too closely linked to the maternal model, and doubles up on what is expected of mothers and what they actually do, and so there is not enough differentiation to give the child the space they need to fully separate from their mothers. The father is not able to become a functional father.

So there are two models of fatherhood, and each turns out to be a disappointment. But why? Both of these models give rise to suffering in one form or another, because some men cannot cope with the dissatisfaction that each of the models has presented to them. Is this why paternal depression is present in some men after they have a child?

These 'new' fathers in particular are struggling to find their identity now the old framework of male and female, and of maternal and paternal, has been torn down, taking with it the role of the father as dominant and leaving most of the childcare to the mother. Fathers feel like they cannot be nebulous any more; there is more expected of them, and yet they fear becoming redundant. A father's solution is to make himself like his partner, to try to stop her becoming more and more 'solid'. Inevitably this also brings back the feelings he had towards his mother and the way in which he saw his father defeated by his mother's solidity. The authoritarian father (model one) does not work well either, since in recent history it has become undesirable to behave this way. One need only to look at figures such as Hitler, Stalin, Castro, Pol Pot, and so on, who were modelled on the authoritarian father and who placed themselves at the head of a nation and were destroyed. They rose to their immense power, says Naouri, by beginning as the 'little father', but did so as a response to the second, and more prevalent, model of fatherhood. These men often gain power through a discourse of equality, but really they want to have a firm hold over everyone, and a violent one if need be.

This is, of course, an unusual way to talk about mothers and fathers, but I think it is interesting to look at it from an evolutionary viewpoint. But where does this leave us? Naouri suggests that there are two options – either these recent changes to gender and parenting in our society are just setting us up for a more permanent change – the problems will be sorted out in time, and this is just a transitional phase. Or, these new fathers (and mothers) will lead us into chaos – things will get worse, and fathers will have no idea how they are supposed to behave and feel.

Naouri goes on to discuss what these ideas surrounding mothers and fathers mean for the couple. The concept of a nebulous father and a solid mother are not compatible, so how can we live together, often married, and bring up families successfully? Naouri suggests that it is a process that progresses slowly as they learn to see each other and relate to each other's way of being. He likens it to a sort of 'blind man's buff' in which both partners develop into a common space, but without really knowing how, or what, they are doing.

What specific contribution does a father make? We have discussed the fact that he is 'nebulous' and the opposite of the solid and unyielding mother, so what does he do specifically in parenting that is useful?

A father's presence helps the baby to see its mother as a separate being – babies initially have no differentiation between themselves and their mothers – this comes later, and the presence of the father helps this to happen. Fathers still have this urgent sexual desire; the mother responds to this, and so is less wholly available to her baby, and less of an 'omnipotent' mother. A mother's attachment to the father will show an infant that the father is the person who makes his or her mother less omnipotent than they had been led to believe. The presence of the father can also drive the development of speech in a child. A mother and child who remain very close to each other develop their own form of language, often without words, and only decipherable to the child and the mother. So, by developing speech, a child is able to create its own distance from the mother, and to communicate with his father, and other people, thus enabling himself to assume his destiny, make his own identity, and to construct his life.

Naouri points out that the mother is very important in this: she has a role to play in allowing the child to see her as less powerful and less important than the child initially thinks. She has to allow herself to be somewhat 'taken over' by the father, and internalise his importance. The function of the father is, really, anything and everything that is perceived by the child as placing a boundary upon the power that the child would place on their mother in the first instance. It is not a simple case of a mother allowing the father physical contact with her, the mother must value her relationship with the father, and be 'satisfied', both sexually and otherwise. This can be difficult in the postnatal period when there is often a diminished sense of satisfaction in the relationship, or if one or both partners happen to be suffering from postnatal depression.

Naouri stresses the importance of re-establishing a couple's sexual relationship early on after giving birth, because it enables the father to remain as his woman's man, and as his mother-woman's man, and to remain desirable even though he is nebulous; which ultimately helps the child. This emphasis on the early resumption of sexual relations will surely annoy many women. Lack of sleep, lack of time, lack of desire, not to mention the physical demands a new baby has on a woman's body, even if she has had a straightforward birth with no complications – these all contribute to a distinct lack of sexual energy many women feel after the birth. Any suggestion that they must get straight back into it, for the benefit of their partner, and ultimately for the benefit of their child is likely to be met with opposition and dismissal at best, anger at worst.

Interestingly, but perhaps not surprisingly, Naouri does acknowledge the fact that couples with children who have no outside support, and little in the way of a social life, are more fragile than those that do. Couples break up all the time, but having a life 'outside' enables the pair to trust each other more fully, and continue to see the other as the person they want to be with, instead of seeing the changed person who 'didn't used to be like this'. When a couple breaks up, children most often stay with their mother, returning her to a position of omnipotence. Fathers often end up with very little in comparison. Some studies advocate that parents should stay together, even if they don't get on. Clearly this will not always work, but, of course, before divorce became much more commonplace, there were many more couples who did stay together, despite the challenges they faced, and were able to find each other again after any period of difficulty.

What does this mean for children? We have already seen the vast amount of research showing how vulnerable children are, and how the moods and behaviours of their parents have a profound effect on them, possibly for the rest of their lives. Perhaps the most important thing, says Naouri, is that children cannot be fooled easily; if the relationship is breaking down, or there are depressions or stresses, or questions over paternity and fatherhood, then the children will know about it; couples need to know when there is something wrong, and seek help – if not for their sake then for the sake of their children. But this is a difficult thing for parents to do, just as it would be difficult for a father suffering from depression to admit that there is a problem, and so, often, parents will try to explain away any behavioural changes in their children by putting them down to the child's age, and hope they clear up on their own. It is guilt that often stops parents getting the help they need early on, and so until this changes there will be an awful lot of needless suffering.

CHAPTER EIGHT

The father as part of a parenting team

The Fatherhood Institute is the UK's fatherhood 'think and do tank'. Their aim is to move us all towards a society that gives all children a strong relationship with their father or father figure. They work towards a fairer society, with men and women valued equally as carers and earners, which they try to achieve through research, reporting, lobbying for political change, and providing training, consultancy and publications for a father-inclusive practice in a wide variety of settings.

In 2012 they piloted a course called 'Family Foundations', which was aimed solely at couples expecting their first baby together, and consisted of pre- and postnatal groups with the aim of enhancing parent and child wellbeing. The main focus of the course was to teach positive co-parenting – which could be described as 'the way parents support each other' – since this has been shown to have an influence on parenting and child outcomes. It also covered areas such as emotions and how a parent might regulate them, temperament, how to promote a secure attachment with the child, and how to practise positive parenting. The course was delivered in a variety of community settings such as hospitals, community centres or religious centres, and consisted of four classes before the birth and four classes afterwards.

The course had been carried out in the USA before the Fatherhood Institute trialled it, and one outcome had been the reduction of PND in both men and women. Furthermore, those who did go on to suffer from PND after the birth were more likely to recover if they had attended the Family Foundations programme. So, clearly this approach works, but it is very difficult to get this attitude and this way of looking at men and women antenatally and postnatally to become more mainstream.

In the UK, Surrey Parenting and Education Support produced an assessment tool to evaluate the mental health and well-being of fathers with children under two-years-old. The interview is intended for use by experienced health-care practitioners, who are able to deliver the questions and listen to the answers in a sensitive, supportive way. Surrey worked with the Fatherhood Institute to produce the tool, which is based on a framework of ante- and postnatal interviews. It was part of a series of guides designed to help agencies develop father-inclusive services, something that the Fatherhood Institute is very much in favour of, and ran for around eighteen months over 2008 and 2009. The assessment tool, in its preliminary discussions, suggested that fathers should be assumed to be involved in their children's lives, even when they are not living with the children's mothers. It is important to make sure non-resident fathers are involved, and important that this is seen as the norm rather than the exception, by both mothers and fathers.

While the tool urges practitioners to challenge fathers who do not engage, it also acknowledges that some mothers may have fears or doubts about their child's father becoming more involved. Practitioners are encouraged to begin by asking men to identify their strengths as fathers, and to say what they think are the positive influences their presence gives to their children and their children's mothers. Information about how fatherhood can be a positive experience and how involvement in their children's lives can be a positive thing should be available to fathers to reinforce this idea.

These sorts of courses and tools provide an ideal opportunity for fathers to be asked about their mental state, and for them to be informed about PND. Fathers who took part acknowledged that some health-care staff do not have the expertise or the capacity to engage with them during home visits; the fathers often feel uncomfortable. The Fatherhood Institute argues forcefully that it is the *couple* that must be the focus of antenatal and postnatal care, not just the mother and baby. The couple will become parents together, and yet one half of the parenting team is ignored by health-care professionals and by society too. It would be beneficial for the couple and therefore the child if health-care services talked to the couple before the birth, and both mothers and fathers would benefit from more information, especially regarding PND. But there simply isn't time or resources for this the way things are currently set up.

Health-care services are very stretched in the UK, and I have already discussed how this also applies to NHS maternity services; pregnant mothers could be given up to ten appointments during their pregnancy. These are often quick, ten minute appointments with a midwife, who is often running behind schedule and has many women to see who depend on her services. According to the NHS website, postnatal depression should be mentioned at the thirty-six week check-up; but only at this one appointment, and it could be as little as giving the mother a leaflet to read after she leaves. Many women see a different midwife is seen at each appointment. There is little or no continuity of care, and the midwife (or sometimes a doctor) is almost exclusively focused on the physical health of the mother and her baby – there simply isn't sufficient time or resources to adequately prepare women for postnatal depression. Fathers, then, haven't got a chance.

Maternity services, clearly, are not father inclusive. Fathers are mentioned, but only in terms of their genetic history, as if this is their only contribution to the child or to the partnership. Jeszemma Garratt, at the Fatherhood Institute, suggests that simple things like having two chairs at a scan or at other appointments would acknowledge the father and might make it more normal to have the father there and seen as an important part of the child's life. As things stand at the moment in maternity care, fathers are superfluous, since nothing would change in the care women receive if the father was not there.

The Fatherhood Institute has also worked on pilot training for health visitors to make sure they mentioned both parents' mood at their postnatal visits, rather than simply going through the necessary parts of the child's 'red book' (England's red book is officially called the Personal Child Health Record – it includes a record of the child's height, weight, vaccinations, and developmental milestones). Without training, it was thought that health visitors would be unlikely to mention or even notice a father's mood. Garratt says that, for many men, it only takes one person to make a difference. It could be a midwife or a friend, but the person who actually asks a father "How are you feeling?" will stick in their mind because it will be so rare.

Some children's centres do have some contact with fathers after a birth and therefore some role in engaging fathers. There are groups specifically for fathers at many centres, usually running on a Saturday morning. There are also some parenting classes and groups available, and all groups (except the breastfeeding group) are open to fathers with babies as well as mothers. So, *if* fathers come to these groups then staff will have a chance to engage with them, and, according to Garratt, there are instances where fathers do report feeling low, or a lack of attachment with their baby if they are asked. But, this is only possible where fathers actually come to a group, and so there is little opportunity for the staff to actually evaluate a father's mental state, or to refer them elsewhere if necessary. Other community centres, such as jobcentres or housing offices, provide other opportunities for fathers to have contact with someone, but the emotional states of *people* are never noticed in these places. As a society we don't see men as emotional beings – and this has wide-ranging consequences – it affects behaviour and influences practice.

Garratt argues that men are not asked about their mood *ever*. In the context of birth and parenting this is true, and it is certainly the case for many fathers and couples. Fathers are forgotten in any discussion of postnatal depression, and so there is little chance that they will be remembered in any other context. This view of men as non-emotional beings is so entrenched that if a man were to present himself somewhere with signs of depression then most staff in a community setting would not know what to do with him. Men *can* be difficult after a baby is born; they can go out drinking too much, they can work long hours at the office, or they can become withdrawn from the family and find it difficult to engage with their new baby, but, no, they cannot be depressed.

Clearly this attitude is damaging and needs to change, both sexes should be seen as emotional beings as a matter of course, so that postnatal depression in fathers is not seen as unusual. As

I have already said, most men would not go to the doctor if they felt depressed. They might not even realise that they are depressed, and so it is vital that all of us, and particularly those staff who work in the community, are adept at noticing the signs of depression and being aware that fathers need to be asked how they are feeling. We also need to make sure we listen to their answer and have clear guidelines in place for what their next steps can be for treatment or further evaluation.

As I have discussed in previous chapters, families are changing, but Garratt points out that family services have not yet caught up and are still working with the traditional and outdated notion that women do the caring, and men do the working. There is still an underlying belief that fathers are not engaged with their children – but this is just a belief, and not a true depiction of the majority of families. Perhaps the sticking point is that we don't see men as carers – our view of them as fathers is that they are more the breadwinning, respected heads of families, when really they are capable of caring as much as women and they *do*. Services also seem to have incorrect information about fathers – Garratt tells me that they believe that only around 60% of fathers are involved in a relationship with their partner at the time of birth, when actually the figure is 96.4%. This misinformation, and the underlying stereotypes that continue to shape our view of genders and their roles in society, leave fathers feeling that services do not want to engage with them. Fathers need to start being seen *as* fathers, not just as breadwinners, or aggressive or unemotional, or any of the other things that are the stereotypical view of a man.

The gender balance in the workforce is changing, but it is still not equal, and many families still do have a father who goes out to work and a mother who stays at home with the children. Really, the attitudes towards each gender who are in the workforce needs to change so that they are seen more equally. Mothers can find themselves labelled as unreliable or given less responsibility than their male colleagues simply because they have returned to work after having a child. In the workplace, fathers are not seen as such; nothing changes for them at work once they have children, and they too may need the flexibility offered to their female colleagues, or even more time off when their child is born.

Although many would agree that this change in attitude is long overdue, it is difficult to translate this into everyday practice. What is needed, and what makes it so difficult, is that this different treatment of men and women is so entrenched and habitual in our society. Changes that we make to our attitudes and to the attitudes of community services and family services have to be done at every level. Fathers have to be thought of as equal to mothers all day, every day, so that it is seen as normal and it becomes the new way that we do things and the way that we see parents, and people, as equal, emotional beings.

As we have seen in the research carried out regarding possible changes to antenatal education, men want to be given the chance to engage on an emotional level with other men, and dads' groups do have a place – certainly there are fathers who want to attend; however, Garratt says that if fathers are only given opportunity to discuss their feelings at fathers' groups then we are moving backwards. Fathers should be treated as part of a couple, and we need to rearrange our ideas and practices so that they are treated as co-parents; in fact, the promotion of a good and supportive relationship is beneficial and can be a protective force against the onset of postnatal depression.

Garratt is adamant that the couple needs to be at the forefront of everyone's mind when they are dealing with a new child, and also when they are dealing with a family; for instance, letters are often addressed to the 'parents' of a child, but names are not given, and so inevitably the mother will end up thinking it is really meant for her, since, as a mother, the childcare is primarily her domain. What needs to happen, says Garratt, is that parents must be addressed together by name, which will help fathers be at the forefront of our minds, rather than placing all parental responsibility on the mother. Garratt also says that the Surrey assessment tool suggests it should be routine that fathers are automatically included in all appointments and meetings to do with the baby, and that appointments need to be available at times that are convenient for both mothers and fathers to attend; this would mean that more evening and weekend appointments would need to be available, which would mean an overhaul of many services and their working arrangements – this is, of course, difficult to implement. Even if the couple do work as a good parenting team, if we don't recognise that such conventions are the norm in society and change that, then sooner or later fathers are going to feel undervalued and unrecognised.

A simple question – "How are you feeling?" If we can make it routine for people to ask that question, though we could really make a difference and it would mean that men can start to be seen as people with feelings. A lot of parenting responsibility is placed on mothers, with fathers usually having responsibility for earning the money and being the head of the family. Not only is this view of families inaccurate, but it also adds to the pressures felt by either sex if they are not fulfilling their perceived roles as they feel they should. If we start to see men as emotional beings, and at the same time start to see women as breadwinners then this will make things easier for both parents, and will be a better representation of society as it stands today.

Many of the healthcare practitioners who took part in the development of the assessment tool were aware of the need for better care for fathers in the peri-natal period. Some said that there was a need for more information to give to fathers, some of whom can seem very vulnerable when they have contact with health visitors etc after a baby is born. Those who took part also acknowledged that some healthcare staff don't have the expertise or the capacity to engage with fathers during home visits, the fathers often seem uncomfortable, and so there is a definite need for, and interest in, training more staff in an assessment tool which would help them to engage fathers and the reasons why this is so important.

All staff who have contact with fathers in the perinatal period should analyse their own attitudes towards men and fathers to ensure that a father-inclusive practice is possible and sustainable, since it is very important that those people who speak to fathers, at every level, are fully on board with these changes. It is important to continually reflect on staff attitudes towards engaging fathers to ensure that it becomes normal and routine to accept them into every appointment and setting.

The Fatherhood Institute has a strong argument for the inclusion of fathers as well as mothers, particularly in maternity services. Their work needs to be more widely acknowledged and taken up by health-care professionals in order to make a real difference to society – it is clear that everyone needs to accept that men, and fathers, are emotional beings too. We need to allow men to have feelings, and feel free to express them so that when their mental health suffers after childbirth they can ask for help and that help can be more widely available. We will not only be helping fathers, but also mothers and entire families. We cannot ignore 50% of the population's emotional needs without facing repercussions.

CHAPTER NINE

Gay fathers, same-sex parents

At the time of writing, marriage between same-sex couples has just become legal in Britain, following several years of civil partnership as the only option for gay couples to have their relationship legally recognised. Full, joint adoption has been legal in England and Wales since 2005, with Scotland following suit in 2009 and Northern Ireland in 2013. The USA has different laws for each state – with regards to same-sex marriage also – but, notably, the state of Rhode Island has allowed all couples to adopt since 1993. Many remain hopeful that more countries will recognise and legalise marriage and adoption for everyone, but we should be aware that parents, even those who are not biologically related to their child, are still vulnerable and *all* fathers can experience some form of postnatal depression. It is also worth remembering that some couples may chose to use a surrogate or a donor, but the result, of course, will still be a baby.

Andrew Solomon is a writer and lecturer on psychology, politics, and the arts, and he is also an activist in LGBT rights and mental health. He lives with his husband and son in New York. He was kind enough to give me some of his views on postnatal depression with regard to same-sex households. He notes that aside from hormonal changes, which happen in both mothers and fathers, the overwhelming responsibility of having a child is a huge factor in postnatal depression. Fathers perhaps feel this responsibility even more than mothers – it hasn't been expected of their sex to prepare for this. Often, in heterosexual couples, the mother does carry out most of the care while the child is an infant. Solomon says that with same-sex couples the responsibilities are usually shared more equally, but there is often one person who does more, or is better at soothing the baby, or quicker to get up in the middle of the night.

Sometimes, says Solomon, neither parent will feel like they are 'better' at caring for the infant; they can both feel incompetent, which can make the couple feel terrible, stressed, and anxious. Fathers are often less prepared for parenthood than mothers, who have grown up with society's expectation that they will fulfil their feminine purpose and have children. Fathers perhaps have less ability to imagine parenthood, and so the shock of becoming a parent can be felt more fully. For couples comprising two fathers, the shock is compounded, and can morph into depression. Negotiation of responsibilities where there is no 'mother' and 'father' can also be tough, and can be an area of conflict. Again, this can be a precursor to postnatal depression.

I wondered if the process of becoming parents in a same-sex couple was a contributing factor to there being more or less postnatal depression among gay couples. Not so, says Solomon, who maintains that it is the stress of parenting and the difficulty in navigating a way through the difficulties that is the 'cause' of postnatal depression. Gay couples don't have accidental pregnancies. A child within same-sex relationships is usually something that has been yearned for 'unconditionally', usually for many years, and a child is usually the result of a very long and drawn-out process. Perhaps that leaves gay couples better prepared for having children, since it is inevitable that the huge responsibility of having a child, and the profound effects it will have on your life, are something gay couples have a lot of time to think about when they make the decision to become parents. The process is a difficult one for a same-sex couple, but it ends with the joy of having a child. "I think life's meaning tends to come from difficult joys, and that the difficulty of having a child within a gay relationship contributes to the joy of doing so," says Solomon.

Same-sex couples, in particular male couples, are in danger of slipping through the net and ending up even more unrecognised than fathers in heterosexual partnerships. There almost certainly won't be any opportunity for them to attend any health-care appointments with the mother of their child, which would only happen in situations where the adoption was arranged before the birth, or perhaps in situations of surrogacy. If they are biologically related to their child then the best they can hope for is to be recognised on the maternity notes and their genetic history to be discussed, but it is worrying that this group of fathers have no real way of being involved. It is important that we don't ignore gay fathers (and non-biological mothers), especially in our evolving society which will become ever more accepting of different family set ups.

Although Andrew Solomon does see that the hard work of having a child can bring enormous reward, it is worth noting that in some situations where the child has been longed for and planned, and it has been a long and difficult journey, there can often be a profound feeling of anticlimax when the baby finally does arrive. It is sometimes seen in couples who go through years of IVF or other fertility treatment; they become depressed after the birth, but feel like they have no right to feel this way, since they should feel lucky to have the child who they worked so hard to have here. Gay fathers, too, can be vulnerable to the dissonance between their expectations of parenthood and the reality.

In situations where the couple has adopted a child, they will have been through a very rigorous process of investigation with much form-filling and assessment over a period of many months. Fathers, like all adoptive parents, can feel like they have to prove that they are worthy, and that they are good enough to be parents, which can be a huge burden to uphold when they do finally get their child. After talking about being a parent and thinking about how great they will be, adoptive parents can be at risk of depression as a result of the high expectations they have of themselves or of the child. These expectations will invariably differ from the reality, which can be very difficult to deal with, particularly on top of the usual things which come with parenting, such as sleep deprivation, lifestyle changes, and relationship changes. Adoptive parents have to realise that no parent can be a super-parent all the time, just as no child can be the perfect child they might have built up in their minds during the adoption process.

It can also be the case that adoptive parents don't feel they get the same recognition that couples get when the mother gives birth to a child. There is no physical sign of an impending baby, since no one is going to be walking around pregnant for nine months. There perhaps won't be the same excitement, and often adoptive parents keep the process private and quiet, since it can sometimes be fragile and uncertain until the last few weeks or even days. Adoptive parents can feel like their experience is less validated than that of birth parents, and that it is forgotten that they are going through the same transition as every biological parent and will be facing the same joys and uncertainties as them too.

There seems to be very few studies that have assessed the

mental health of gay male parents. Dr Abbie Goldberg of Clark University carried out a study in 2010 that focussed on depression and anxiety changes in couples during the first year after adopting a baby. Of the ninety couples studied, thirty-eight were in same-sex relationships. Interestingly, but perhaps not surprisingly, the results showed that the mental health of same-sex couples is affected by their wider social environment – specifically the 'gay-friendliness' of their immediate surroundings. Factors such as anti-gay adoption laws, support from their workplaces, family and friends, and the health of their relationship within their partnership all affected the incidence of depression and anxiety.

The study was carried out in the USA, where each state has different adoption laws regarding gay couples, and it was noted that couples living in states where there were anti-gay laws experienced greater levels of anxiety and depression. Certainly there are still different attitudes found in Western society towards same-sex couples, with a significant proportion feeling negatively towards them with little acceptance of their presence in society.

The level of support offered to same-sex parents will inevitably be dictated by the attitudes of the society in which it is offered. Happily, acceptance of gay couples as parents feels like it is on the increase, and films and television programmes all play a part in showing sceptics that gay parents are just as able to provide a loving, stable, two-parent home, just as well as heterosexual couples can. Although a move in the right direction, it is somewhat sad that our attitudes are reliant on what we are shown by the media, instead of accepting same-sex couples for what they are and offering them the same rights and services as all parents.

CHAPTER TEN

The first year of fatherhood

What can men expect from fatherhood? And is there any way of preparing them for that before it actually happens? Men may have friends or family members who are fathers before they are, or they might have read a book, or seen fathers and their babies on the television, or in the park, or in the supermarket, but nothing can really, truly prepare them. It is something that can only be learned through actually being a father, and every experience will be different, with a different set of circumstances and with different partners with different personalities and expectations. But even though it is a unique experience, there are certain themes that run through every father's experience, and next I will explore twelve of these themes based on insights from the many fathers I know, as well as the findings of a study carried out in 2007 in Sweden, which interviewed ten fathers, in depth, in the second year of their first child's life.

1. Feeling overwhelmed

Becoming a father has often been described, by fathers themselves, as an overwhelming event. It is a positive experience, something that is looked forward to for months, sometimes years, but it completely changes a person's life. It really does completely take over – it is one of the biggest changes that can occur, and it can be very difficult to adjust to this new set of circumstances. People often struggle with putting someone else before themselves in almost all aspects of life – and nothing can prepare you for it. Parents are sent home from the hospital with a helpless being they are wholly responsible for. Mothers perhaps have some idea as to what they should be doing, but it is certainly a shock to be woken throughout the night or to have to spend a whole day feeding a hungry newborn. Most fathers are very glad of being able to take paternity leave – in this country a father is entitled to one or two weeks' paid paternity leave or, more recently, a father can take an additional twenty-six weeks' paid leave, but only if the mother (or co-adopter) returns to work.

The fact that fathers recognise leave as important is a reflection of how they feel about promoting a good relationship with their child, and of just how unique and important the occasion of a new child entering the family is. Some of the fathers I have talked to find paternity leave quite a difficult time though, and even though they want to be around their partner and their new baby, it can be easier for them to return to work. As we have seen in this book, some men don't want to be around their new family and find it very difficult to adjust to being a father.

2. Difficult to prepare for

An overwhelming life event, then, is something very difficult to prepare for, but antenatal classes do try to do just that for expectant parents. It has certainly been acknowledged that antenatal education needs to be adjusted to better meet the needs of fathers, and so it is not surprising that the fathers in the Swedish study found their own antenatal education lacking, and of questionable value. The main focus of these classes is the mother – this does seem natural, since they will be the ones going through it, but for fathers this is not very relevant, and many would prefer there to be some information more focused on them. Most antenatal classes concentrate, of course, on the mother and the birth – the mechanics, the pain relief options available, and the possible complications and scenarios that could arise. While this is useful, and it helped to remind some fathers in the study that anything could happen and that they had little control over it, many of them said that they couldn't remember what they were taught and couldn't describe the benefits of it at all – it was just something they were expected to attend and so they did without much further thought. Some fathers saw the classes as a way to prepare mentally for fatherhood, but found that they had been overlooked somewhat in the group – again backing up the idea that there needs to be separate classes to enable both sexes to get what they each specifically need from antenatal education.

Many fathers feel that there is not enough preparation for how life with a newborn will be – simple things like basic childcare, feeding, sleeping, etc. – would be useful for both mothers and fathers. Often there are postnatal education groups, but since they often take place after the child is here and in the daytime, the father is usually back at work, or if they are not, they are usually the only father at the class. So, fathers feel a bit left out once the baby arrives; their lives have changed, there has been this overwhelming event, but they don't feel like there has been enough focus on them in all the preparations. Lack of sleep and high expectations are both things that concern new fathers – even if they are not expected to get up with the baby during the night they will often be woken and won't be used to the disturbance to their sleep.

Similarly, they will not be used to the additional things expected of them, such as the expectation to not only provide for their family, but also be an active participant in helping their partner care for their baby. Interestingly, many fathers do like talking to other new or expectant fathers because they have this huge life changing event in common, so, again, there is a lot of evidence for male oriented antenatal classes to run alongside the more traditional female ones.

3. The baby's needs coming first

When people become parents they quickly realise that the baby takes the central position in the family. Fathers are less free to do as they please, and there is less time for leisure activities at the weekend and in the evening. Of course in some partnerships the father is still able to go out and do whatever he did before; the expectations and needs of the mother will differ, depending on the relationship. Most fathers who are involved in family life reported feeling irritated, sometimes, that there was very little room for spontaneity; the baby's eating and sleeping times tend to be the main focus of the day, and things are planned around these events. Often the mother is the one 'in charge' of this schedule, since she is the primary carer, and so many fathers feel like they have to check and plan activities with their partner and get their 'permission' to see that they fit in with the baby. This can be difficult for some fathers – to hand over control of family time to their partners – but the men in the study did not seem concerned that this was now the dynamic in their families.

Interestingly, fathers were happy to join in with baby-centred activities, especially if they were the kind of activities that were amusing for the child, like a baby music class, or a soft play centre, for instance. Fathers are less keen to do things with the baby that aren't as active or involved for the child – meeting up with friends at a coffee shop or library, or going to other parents' houses when the baby is young is not something many fathers enjoy.

Fathers have to change their priorities when they have a baby, meaning that hobbies and leisure activities often need to be postponed so that they can spend time with the baby, although the amount of rearranging differs widely from father to father. Some felt that they needed to speed up current projects, such as a house renovation, so that they could spend time with their child later on, while others felt that it could be put off for a few months or years while the child takes priority. Of course the actual experience of fathers varies, but it is certain that the baby will have to take centre stage during the first year of its life, and, to some extent, things will have to be rearranged.

Many fathers are surprised, at first, by how much needs to be done in order to leave the house, and how much organisation it can take. There is a lot to think about when you have an extra person to leave the house with, and babies are often a shock to fathers, and parents in general, in this regard.

4. Fathers' need to remain the same person

Prioritising a child brought up all sorts of feelings for new fathers in their first year of fatherhood. Some men find it difficult to put a child first, while some can adapt to the new family dynamic very easily. Former interests and hobbies are important to a lot of new fathers, who feel that although some things *have* to change, it is very important to retain a sense of who they are, and who they were before their child came along. For most men though, this realisation highlights the need for mothers to do the same, and to have some time 'off' from being a parent also. Often this results in parents taking turns to care for the baby so that the other can go and do their own thing for a few hours. There will be occasions when the baby will have to be part of some of the things a couple would have done before the baby was around, like taking holidays and going to restaurants. Of course, this can be stressful, and some parents will think it's impossible to bring a baby wherever you go, but it certainly *can* be done, without the couple sacrificing their need to retain some sense of themselves. and their identity from before they had children. The fathers in the Swedish study realised that if they felt happy and content, then the baby would also feel happy and content – perhaps not all fathers realise this, and the acknowledgment of this fact would be of use in convincing depressed fathers to seek help. Not all fathers would be so self-aware, or aware of the effect their mood has on their child.

5. New discoveries about themselves

Many fathers are surprised by the feelings and traits that a new baby can awaken in them. Fathers often feel that they want to get involved and master new situations, like getting the baby to sleep or comforting it when it cries. Many fathers want to be able to handle the baby and feel confident in their own abilities when the mother is not around – this provides an enormous amount of satisfaction, and it also shows them different sides to their personalities, which may have lain dormant up until fatherhood.

Personalities can become enriched with calmness, patience and sensitivity when a baby arrives, and these traits often extend to other areas, even when the father is not caring for the baby. For instance, many fathers report feeling sad watching films where something sad affects a child – this wouldn't have happened before fatherhood for most men.

Most of all, fathers report feeling like they have to 'grown up' once they enter fatherhood; like they have to be mature and ready to put the baby first, and this attitude often makes them better at interpreting the baby's actions and figuring out what they want.

6. Being responsible

Fathers do feel the sudden and overwhelming responsibility of fatherhood in terms of giving the child a secure home life. Providing for the family is a very traditional view of fatherhood, where the man is expected to go out and work, but it is one that persists in our society, especially during a child's first year. Fathers may have less money to spend on themselves, since the breadwinning duties will often fall solely on them, and so they might feel resentful of this. Responsibility can also be felt as a need to take extra care of themselves and to take fewer risks so that their baby will continue to be provided for, and many fathers report this change in attitude and behaviour in the first year of their baby's life. One thing that hits fathers is just how fragile and helpless their baby is, and this triggers a strong need to protect him or her, and the mother too, from the potentially harmful outside world.

Fathers also wanted to spend time with their child and sometimes tried to work shorter days in order to achieve this, but often this was not possible. It is common for fathers to get home from their working day after a baby has been put to bed, so time spent with their baby is limited to weekends. This highlights how difficult it can be to combine providing for the family with being an involved father. For some men this can be quite overwhelming and a source of pressure.

Fathers often felt a new sense of responsibility as a consequence of how other people saw them. A new baby is certainly something that people comment on, and strangers, friends and relatives would see the father in a new light, and have certain expectations of their behaviour. Night wakings were considered one of the most difficult and demanding parts of fatherhood, and some men enjoyed getting sympathy from colleagues and friends, which helped them to feel responsible, and also helped them feel like they were able to master their new role if they could do these demanding things as well as their partners. Men who, for some reason, were unable to care for the baby at some point during its first year often felt bad and 'insufficient' as fathers, though it seems more common for fathers to feel that they can handle the situation and its demands.

7. The strain of having a new baby

Of course, having a baby is a huge strain on parents, physically, mentally, and emotionally. There are several aspects of parenting that fathers, in particular, find a source of strain.

Sometimes fathers feel that the quality of the childcare provided by others, presumably when their partner is not available, is not good enough, but they cannot provide the childcare themselves because they are at work, and so this makes them worried and anxious that their child is not being looked after as best as it could be. This is probably something that fathers feel unable to express much of the time, and because they have a new responsibility (the child), they must continue to work and to provide for them, and so the childcare situation remains the same whether they like it or not.

Some new fathers feel like there is not much support for them– no guidelines specifically for dads, no role models, or perhaps no family members they can turn to for advice; they may be the first in their group of friends to become a father. This perhaps highlights how little men talk to each other about parenting and fatherhood, and how much they need to. This is particularly important, since many fathers fear being isolated once their baby arrives. The huge demands an infant places on a parent's time are unimaginable, and often fathers don't realise how demanding an infant would be or how 'non-social' they could be either. Certainly in the first year a baby can be difficult to fit into the life a father had before, and so they worry that they will be cut off from friends and from the world because everything will revolve around the baby. This can be a source of unhappiness for fathers, and because they aren't used to talking about it with their peers, men can feel cut off for quite some time. This also adds to the worries some men feel about their competence in being a parent, and most men compare themselves to their partner in this regard and feel inferior.

Fathers also feel that the changes to their relationship that occur with the birth of the baby are a source of stress and worry during the first year of fatherhood. Some men feel like their partners don't have any feelings left for them after caring so much for the baby, and feel they are no longer the focus of their partner's love, which in turn can leave them emotionally unstable – they no longer feel secure in their partner's love. Sex is also a source of sadness for new fathers, since it is inevitable that a couple's sex life will be less active for a while.

8. Completeness

It sounds cliché, but, really, many fathers report feeling a new completeness in life once they have become a father and become a family. Some men describe it as a sort of wholeness. A close relationship with the child is an expression of the relationship a man has with his partner, and for many this gives a feeling of comfort and satisfaction.

9. Being close to the baby

It is important to fathers that they become close to their child in its first year. For most fathers this starts with organising paternity leave to ensure they are around at the beginning. Some men in the Swedish study had problems getting their employer to agree to paternity leave at all, but there are some European countries where fathers are entitled to a lot more leave than in the UK. There are a few reports among fathers here of it being difficult for them to take time off, whether it is because of the way work is structured or because of the nature of the work they do. It can also be difficult for families financially during paternity leave, since statutory paternity pay is minimal. (In 2014, statutory pay was a maximum of £138.18 per week, which would equate to an annual salary of just over £7,000. Clearly this is a vast pay cut for many fathers, even if it is only for a few weeks.)

Fathers often have limited contact with their new baby in its first few weeks while their partner is establishing breastfeeding. It can make a father feel less bonded to their child, since they are aware of the powerful intimacy between the mother and child that this act gives them, while also being all too aware of how little close contact they get in comparison. Obviously if the baby is bottle fed there are more opportunities for sharing feeding duties. And once the father is back to work their time with the baby is usually limited again. A lot of fathers have reported spending more time with their child as it grew older and feeling happy that the mother didn't have such a monopoly over them. It is natural for a baby to want to be with its primary carer, and in very few cases is this the father, and so when it happens that the baby is happy to be with its father, many dads feel special and truly like a 'father'.

Many fathers are excited to witness their child developing and growing day by day, and express their feelings for their child as abundant with love and happiness. Even fathers who experienced difficult nights or other demands found that their baby gave them warmth and affection at other times, which made up for it. Most fathers found that they were attentive to their children and enjoyed caring for them.

Sometimes mothers or other family members take over, leaving it difficult for the father to get involved at all. Fathers who face this situation are often sad and hurt that they can't get as close to their child as they would like to, and they feel excluded because of the close bond the child has with the mother. Although this is not unpredictable – men will know that the mother will have a closer bond to the child than they will – it is nevertheless a shock to some new fathers, who didn't expect to feel so distressed about being more distant from the child than they wanted to be. Some fathers, though they are there in a given situation, are pushed away by their partners, who take over all the care for the baby; not allowing the father to rock the baby to sleep or comfort them. This is, of course, very difficult for a father, and, although unusual, probably goes unnoticed and isn't talked about, since mothers are usually the primary carers in the first year and are expected to do the lion's share of childcare and childrearing.

10. Better relationship with partner

Fathers often report a new affinity in their relationship after their baby is born, even though the arrival means that the couple spend less time together. The greater calmness and depth in the relationship helps fathers to understand what their partner is going through, and to understand their partner's need for rest and leisure time – which is often seen as vital to maintaining a good relationship. Fathers do often want to share the baby's care equally, but of course this is dependent on work patterns. Even so, many fathers view parenting as a partnership, and feel good that their partner allows them to take responsibility as a father. In This is something which is very important for fathers to expect from the first year of fatherhood. It will give fathers confidence in their new role if they go into it knowing they are in an equal relationship, and, at the same time, it will benefit mothers in having a partner who wants to take equal responsibility for their new baby.

Fathers wanted to discuss how their child was to be brought up and cared for with their partners, with the aim of agreeing on certain methods and arrangements. Many fathers report that this is a source of conflict in the relationship, but that most of the time a mutual agreement was reached. Fathers often fight to make their opinions about upbringing heard, even though they often do less of the day to day care; it is important for them to have their say and feel like an equal parent. Fathers also reported a beneficial change in the relationship with their own parents, often seeing more of them and enjoying watching the new grandparent-grandchild relationship develop.

11. Reflection on your own life

When any life-changing event takes place it is not unusual for a person to really examine their own life and take stock. Fathers often feel a sort of deadline to 'sort themselves out' once their children have been born; it can mean that men re-examine their morals, values, and behaviour, and inconsistency or hypocrisy is picked up as they apply their previous standards of behaviour to their new situation. The changes are usually wide-ranging, from making their lifestyle healthier to taking better care of themselves, trying to be a less angry, or a more hardworking person, or be happier with who they have become.

Fathers may look back at how they were raised and use their own experiences as a basis for how they want to be as a father. One father I spoke to could remember his parents telling him off a lot of the time, and it made him remember the injustice he felt, and the sadness too, and so he vowed never to shout at his children. Another couldn't remember his father ever playing with him and his siblings, and so will always make the effort to spend time playing with his child. There are positive aspects fathers take from their own upbringing too, such as little things their fathers involved them with, or how they spoke to them.

Fathers naturally look at their children and think about

CHAPTER ELEVEN

Real experiences of PPND

As part of my research I was fortunate enough to track down some men who were willing to share their stories – something infinitely useful and reassuring for those who are going through PPND or have gone through it or something similar is to know they are not alone. Names have been changed along with any identifying details.

Paul's worries about becoming a father started before his partner had the baby. It was an unexpected pregnancy since his girlfriend was told she had poly-cystic ovaries and might have difficulty conceiving. In actual fact, the couple conceived within six weeks of stopping birth-control pills.

"Initially we were really surprised," says Paul, "and we couldn't believe it had happened so quickly. For about a day I was excited, but then the reality sunk in, and I realised there was nothing I could do now, it was all out of my control and we were going to have a baby. A child! I was up and down, sometimes thinking I'd be ok and feeling happy and excited, and then suddenly down, and then up again, and then I felt really down and never really recovered from it. I was suffering from anxiety, probably quite severely, and I went to the doctor who put me on antidepressants, which I have taken in the past, but hadn't for about five years. I felt really out of control – all my friends were having babies, with most of them on to their second or third, and while I wanted them too, the choice had been taken away from me – so I felt really conflicted. I *did* want kids, but I was having all these negative feelings and feeling so anxious. I come from a traditional family and so I had to think about making a proper commitment to my girlfriend because it's the right thing to do. But I kept also having lots of bad, awful thoughts, which I'm ashamed of – like hoping she miscarried the baby, or wanted to get rid of it. I felt like I was in a desperate situation and couldn't get out. I really wanted to stop feeling like that. It was really stressful and upsetting."

Paul had an advantage, since he had identified the source of his feelings before the baby was born – this would be the kind of man who would benefit from a programme like the one Adam Jukes attempted to set up in Chapter Three.

Neil, who was in his mid-thirties when he had his first child with his wife, also experienced some of the anxiety Paul suffered. These men are unusual in that they do link their behaviour and feelings to the pregnancy of their partner; this is by no means a small accomplishment, but it is not widespread.

"We were under a lot of stress anyway, my wife works away a lot with her job and she'd just been told she was going to a job about a hundred miles away from where we live. I had quit my job (with her backing) to find something better, which would fulfil me more, but it took a long time, and I was still unemployed when we found out about the baby. From the moment we found out she was pregnant my stress levels went through the roof. I was so concerned with my employment situation, I wondered if I would ever be able to provide for my family again – my wife's job is excellent, but she was going to have to take time off for the baby and I didn't know how we were going to cope. I lost weight, I couldn't sleep, I had pains in my stomach – I was a mess. I would be embarrassed to admit to anyone that I broke down in tears on a few occasions. I could never tell anyone that who knew me.

I was also so worried about how the relationship with my wife would change, and I was pissed off too, that we were going to have to forget about some of our dreams – some of the stuff we really had wanted to do with our lives. I just felt really worthless."

Neil eventually sought help from his GP, but had he not, those problems and fears would have continued after the birth. From what he tells me about his wife, their relationship might not have survived had he not been proactive and aware enough to admit he had a problem.

Another father who had the same clarity of mind to seek help was Abraham. His is quite an extreme example, and it is worth noting that this sort of experience is incredibly rare. However, Abraham was lucky because his partner took charge and helped him to get the help he needed. Again, not everyone has a solid relationship to begin with, but in this case it saved Abraham's life.

"I was fine for the whole pregnancy. We had been trying for a baby for a few months and we were both so excited that it had happened and we would become parents. Then about three or four weeks before our son was born I had some experiences which really shocked me – I would suddenly get these thoughts, really awful things, about my wife, like doing bad things to her and bad things happening. I also started crying excessively, so I stopped going out if I felt I couldn't control it. I work from home, so it was easy to hold it in, but it started to scare me – especially the thoughts. They turned into something more like 'voices' – and to be honest I was petrified. I didn't dare tell anyone – the voices were so intrusive, aggressive, even, and they really upset me. I knew it wasn't like me, you know, to think these things, but the thoughts were still there, and I was scared. It got worse really quickly, and then I started going around thinking that every single thing that happened to me was happening for a reason – something as simple as talking to a man in a shop, or listening to the radio, and then I thought that maybe they were trying to tell me to run away because this wasn't my life any more – I wasn't meant to have a child. In the midst of this – and I was suicidal – my son was born. I was so overwhelmed with anger, confusion, sadness, and nostalgia, I just couldn't handle it. I was such a shit father. I lost nearly a stone in weight – I didn't eat – and I just didn't participate at all in being a dad. One day I totally lost it and had a crazy panic attack in front of my wife – and I am so grateful she was there because she made me see someone about what I was going through. I saw a psychiatrist who prescribed me an antipsychotic drug as well as antidepressants. I finally began to feel better – it was such a slow process, but I could enjoy being a dad.

It was weird. I *knew* I loved my wife and son, but I couldn't understand why I had been so fucked up in those first few weeks and the weeks before the birth. Honestly, I wish I'd talked about it the minute it started so I didn't have to be such a shit person in my son's first few weeks. I really lost understanding of everything. I don't think I could have gone on much longer if my wife hadn't stepped in."

Some fathers struggle with the new demands of fatherhood.

"My baby is a year old now, and I have only just begun to

put into words how I'm feeling. I don't even know if it's related to past issues or if it's to do with his birth. I sometimes feel so inadequate and hopeless. I feel like I'm failing, like I'm not connected to anything around me, which makes me feel so isolated, and even more hopeless and inadequate.

"I should say that my wife and I had difficulties in getting pregnant in the first place, and it took nearly six years, with several losses and medical interventions along the way. I'm not sure I ever dealt with those feelings, I think I was so focused on supporting my wife that I neglected my own anger and sadness at the situation."

Some mothers might relate to the following account, although they might be surprised to learn it is a father talking about his feelings following his child's birth:

"I can deal with being tired. Surely we all have to deal with being tired at some point in our lives. But I have no time to do anything I enjoy – it's a constant routine of work, dinner, deal with screaming baby, restless sleep, repeat. Even at the weekends I never seem to be able to break this routine. I feel like I have no real choices in my life, since I can't deviate from this path now.

"I know depression runs in my family, and I know I should speak to a doctor about this, but I just feel so ashamed. Shouldn't I just 'man up' and deal with it? Doesn't everyone have to deal with this when they have a baby? I never imagined having a baby would make me feel so unhappy and hopeless."

Another, similar story:

"I wake up every morning feeling sad and anxious, it lasts a few hours, then by afternoon I feel ok. Sometimes I feel down in the evenings too. My wife is due to give birth to our first child in a few months and I keep fearing that I will lose my job, even though there's not really any chance of that happening. I thought maybe I was burned out and needed to change jobs, but again, I don't think that's really going to happen, and I don't think it's the reason I'm feeling so down, but I'm not sure what is.

I went to my GP who said that I was putting the stress and anxiety about the pregnancy and fatherhood onto other parts of my life, but I can't really identify with that. I feel happiest when I'm around my wife and our unborn baby, so how can that be right? I just feel so confused about why I am feeling this way. The doctor put me on a dose of antidepressants. I really hope these feelings don't continue after the baby is born.

Another new dad shares his experience here:
"Before we had our son I was really into loads of stuff, I had lots of hobbies; I was always on the go – motorcycling, photography, surfing, musician and marathon runner. My wife and I used to travel every year and we've visited many countries.

We tried for years to have kids – maybe three years with no luck. After that my wife quit her job to lower her stress levels, since we thought that maybe it was affecting her ability to get pregnant. Then, after another year, we decided to stop the fertility medication, and then after a couple of months we found out she was pregnant.

"I thought I would really enjoy fatherhood, but I think I thought I could just do it for a few hours a day then go back to my motorbikes or running. But obviously I can't do that, I just go to work every day and then come home to my wife and the baby. We aren't intimate any more, and I am incredibly sexually frustrated.

I am also experiencing a lot of issues with anger. I have

had problems dealing with anger in the past, but I have always channelled my energies into my hobbies – like going for a run when I feel the rage – and now I can't do that, so I have started to let it out at home."

A common precursor for PND in mothers is a traumatic birth. A percentage of births do lead to an unplanned caesarean section, sometimes as an emergency, or intervention with forceps, ventouse, or an episiotomy. Sometimes procedures need to be performed very quickly; sometimes the baby's heart rate is cause for concern, or maybe there are problems with the labouring mother, such as dangerously high blood pressure. The support for mothers after these births is often non-existent, or at best it has to be sought – for instance some hospitals offer a 'de-briefing' by a midwife afterwards if it is unclear why things panned out the way they did. This can help a woman come to terms with the trauma of a difficult birth, which is a huge amount to deal with emotionally as well as physically. There is no such provision for fathers, who have often witnessed the whole thing and so can be emotionally traumatised too; it is therefore no wonder that some fathers experience depression.

Here, three other fathers share their stories:

"My son was born under very traumatic circumstances. My wife had been in labour for twelve hours before she was rushed into theatre for an emergency caesarean. There were complications during the surgery and I thought I would lose my wife – after they got the baby out she had to have another three hours of surgery to save her life and they put her to sleep so fast that she didn't even get to hold our newborn son. She was in the hospital for a further week and a half until we were told we could go home.

"Since then our relationship has really suffered. We have been through a lot; we have moved house twice because I was made redundant – my new job was in a different part of the country and we ended up making a huge loss on the sale of the house, which has put us heavily into debt. We had no one around to lean on, no family, no friends, since they were all back home where we had moved from. I know my wife really struggled with not having any friends close by.

"I work very long hours so that we don't get even further into debt, and because of this I am tired all the time and have no energy or motivation to do anything when I'm not at the office. I don't even want to chase around after my son, and it worries me that my tiredness is affecting our relationship. He doesn't often want me to do things for him, like put him to bed or give him dinner or a bath – and that makes me feel sad – he just wants his mummy, and I don't blame him. My wife has started to be reluctant to leave me alone with our son, saying I am clumsy and seem like I don't know what I'm doing when she sees me with him. But I know she's always watching me and so I'm always on edge and that's probably the reason I seem so 'clumsy'. On the rare occasions that I am alone with my son I stop doubting myself and feel like I am doing ok.

"My wife was with the health visitor and was talking about me – she seems to think I have some sort of paternal postnatal depression as a result of everything that has happened in the last year. I suppose it would explain my lack of motivation and lack of energy and enjoyment in general. It might also be an explanation for the headaches and migraines that I have recently been prescribed some very heavy medication for. It's hard to admit to it, as a man, and I'm not sure what my next steps should be to try and sort myself out. I don't want to break up my family."

"We had our first child, a boy, last year. My wife suffered from PND at first and it took a few months for her to really feel attached to him. I tried to be understanding, but it got to me, and I became really frustrated with her and with 'us' for not being the couple we used to be. We just didn't communicate at all, and I felt guilty that I couldn't make my wife better and I couldn't fix the situation.

"I started to have nightmares in the first few months after our son was born. I told my wife, and she and I assumed it was as a result of his birth. It started off really well, really natural, but ended in a C-section, which was unexpected and pretty stressful. As well as the nightmares I would have panic attacks about my son's safety and well-being, and I'd panic that he was in some sort of terrible danger or pain. He wasn't, but I would be left with all that adrenalin and I often couldn't calm down for hours.

I keep feeling really guilty about my son's birth, even though I know it was totally out of my control. I just really wanted her to have the natural birth we had imagined. I feel like I need to control every other aspect of my life in order to make up for it somehow, and I always want things done a certain way or I get really stressed and panicky. I don't think I have properly taken the time to process what happened."

"The pregnancy was fine, absolutely no problems, but the labour was awful. She was labouring on and off for four days, and straight after the baby was born she was taken away to the special care unit and we didn't get to take her home for a week. Initially I was fine. I loved it, and we had loads of visitors, so the house was busy – everyone said what a great dad I was being. I even thought I'd like to stay at home with the baby while my wife went to work!

"After a week or so I started having these awful thoughts.

They were really upsetting, like the baby dying, getting ill, having an awful life or something bad happening to her to mess her up. I went back to work after a fortnight and put in some really long days but I couldn't sleep properly. I would just lie there thinking these awful thoughts, and then during the day I didn't want anything to do with the baby. I would make an excuse and leave the room if she needed something and I left everything up to my wife to deal with. Eventually I had to confess all of this to my wife – I just broke down in tears in front of her, convinced she'd leave me because of it.

"I went to the doctor's and was prescribed diazepam and something else for anxiety, but I had to go back pretty soon as I wasn't feeling any better, then they gave me some antidepressants. They also put my name down for a referral to see a counsellor. I wish it had never happened, but I am glad I am finally getting some help."

Another story of depression following a traumatic birth – this time told from a mother's perspective:

"I had such a perfect pregnancy. I felt so good for most of it, apart from a little morning sickness at the beginning, and I read so many books on labour that I thought I had it all planned out. However, after fourteen hours of labour the baby's heart rate was worryingly low and we were told I would need an emergency caesarean. It was horribly frightening, and we genuinely thought we'd lost her when she was born and there was no crying to be heard. Eventually, we heard her, and the relief and gratitude was immense.

Luckily, the baby only needed to stay in the special care unit for two days, and we were allowed to go home when they realised there weren't any further issues. I had difficulties at home too, with feeding, mainly, and I got depressed very quickly. The health visitor was fantastic, though, and made sure I was referred to the GP, who got me to a counsellor. It took a few months of darkness and unhappiness, but through hard work and determination I got through it and after six or seven months I felt ok again. My husband was fantastic when I was depressed. He took on so much of the household chores at home and did so much with our daughter, like changing nappies and getting up in the middle of the night when I could not. But we saw less and less of each other, as he also had a full-time job and we got little time to talk.

"I noticed that he seemed to be acting as if he was restless all the time. I could see the tension in his body, and he would get really agitated if she cried and he couldn't settle her quickly. He began to spend more and more time in front of his computer in the evenings, and after a while I realised he was drinking over a bottle of wine a night by himself. He complained about being tired almost all the time, and he became withdrawn and remote. I felt angry with him for being like this when I was just back to my old self, and we had some awful arguments where we both said some terrible things. During one particularly horrible fight he confessed that he hated himself. He felt like a failure for not protecting his family and looking after them like he should. He loved our daughter, but blamed her for wrecking our lives, but he was also terrified she'd think he was a bad father and a bad person.

I made some calls and got him a referral to a psychologist, and we had some counselling together to sort out our crumbling relationship. It has taken a long time, but we are finally both happy."

Here are some more stories told from a mother's perspective:

"My husband was fine with our first two babies, although with my first I had really terrible PND. It took a while for me to recognise it as such, even though I knew something was wrong, but once I had admitted to it I went to the GP and was eventually referred to a psychologist who helped me enormously.

"We both made the decision to have another baby, our third, but when I actually fell pregnant my husband wasn't happy about it. He didn't even smile when I told him the news, and he was different for the whole pregnancy. He never talked about the baby; never even mentioned it, and never rubbed my bump or anything like he did with the other two.

"It was the same after our son was born. He never smiled and he never cried. I had to beg him to hold him so I could have a shower at the hospital. He wouldn't change a nappy or cuddle him. His behaviour was so unusual that it was noticed by the health visitor, and she asked to talk to him alone. It eventually emerged that he was suffering from PND and he blamed everything that had gone wrong with my health in our first pregnancy on the baby. He just couldn't bond with him. Once he started to open up about how he was feeling things started to improve, and two years on he has a great relationship with his son."

"I have been suffering from PND and now my husband's behaviour is making me feel worse. He goes out a lot and doesn't seem to want to be around me and the baby much – he prefers working, or playing computer games, or even going for a bike ride. Anything to get away from us! I can understand it is difficult for him. I often get quite tearful because of the PND, and I don't feel like I cope very well at all, so maybe he doesn't want to be around me in this state. I just feel so alone, and I am starting to really resent him."

"My partner and I had a baby a few months ago. It was

completely planned, and we've been together for five years, and always talked about wanting kids together. It did happen really quickly, so was actually a bit of a surprise, but we were both really happy about it.

Once the baby arrived I got really bad, debilitating postnatal depression. Luckily, my health visitor was really pro-active and got me an appointment at the doctors, and I got the help I needed to get better. Now, nearly a year on, I feel much better, and fully bonded with the baby, but the other day my partner told me he felt like he hadn't really 'warmed' to the baby. He says how difficult he is finding it, how boring the baby is, and how he hates all the crying and the changes we've had to make to our lifestyles. I think he seems a bit depressed.

He does *want* to enjoy the baby. I've seen him make an effort, like getting up at weekends, putting him to bed by himself, etc., but he just doesn't enjoy it at all, and really isn't bonding with him. I know it's supposed to take longer for fathers to bond with their children, but I don't think this is normal."

Some men experience quite extreme physical symptoms as a result of depression after the birth of their child. Here is another story:

"My wife had a very long labour with our son. Overall it went on for about a week and by the end of it we were both absolutely exhausted. After he was born I had to run into the bathroom to be sick, which I put down to lack of sleep and maybe just a reaction to all the excitement. I went home to have a sleep, leaving my wife and baby at the hospital, and my mother came to the house to help make things ready for when we took the baby home. I woke up from my nap really disoriented and confused and started to panic, not knowing what was going on, and feeling really out of control I shouted for help. My mother came in to find me in tears and wanting to run away from my wife and the baby. I felt so overwhelmed. I felt like I just could not be a father. Somehow she calmed me down, and I put it out of my mind and went back to the hospital.

"For the next few months I would wake up every morning feeling anxious, sick, and with a burning feeling in my stomach. I had an upset stomach pretty consistently since the birth, and often I felt like I had to vomit. I would feel anxious when the baby cried, and sometimes even when he didn't, and I would get these awful sick feelings throughout the day. Often I would feel better by the end of the day, but every morning would be the same as the last, with the awful anxiety taking over my mind and body.

"I finally saw a doctor when my wife realised something was desperately wrong. I lost lots of weight as I couldn't eat unless I forced something down, often not until the evening when I felt a bit better. The doctor prescribed me an antidepressant and some tranquilisers for when I felt really awful, but to be honest, these have only addressed the physical symptoms. The anxiety is still there in my head and it's stopping me having the right sort of relationship with my son."

Karl is in his late twenties. His wife, Joy, tells her story here – she is unsure he would ever have talked about it, and they have only ever discussed it very briefly. It does give an insight into how men affect their partners when they don't deal with pregnancy, and he displays many of the classic symptoms, so it is a useful example.

"He was totally on board initially. We hadn't planned it, but we weren't exactly trying to prevent it, if you see what I mean. Then he suddenly wanted me to terminate the pregnancy, which I was not at all willing to do, let alone consider. I hated him for even saying it.

Karl works in a very competitive industry, where long hours are the norm, and he sees clients out of office hours on a regular basis – he is nearly always home late and he worked even harder once we found out about the baby. I didn't mind, I didn't really connect it to the pregnancy to begin with, I just thought he had a lot going on. He has always been proud of making lots of money, too, and I think he was even more obsessed knowing we were going to have a family – he was working and working. I asked him what was going on after a while, since he hadn't said they had new clients or anything, and he does usually tell me about work – he got all angry, thinking I was trying to stop him working and going out – banging on about how I was taking his freedom away from him. Of course this was all in the context of him working late, but it obviously had lots to do with the baby taking away his freedom too.

The thing is, I am always scared about how to approach things like this with him. He had a bad relationship with his mother, and I'm pretty sure he was abused – we don't talk about it much, but he once said he would be scared about one of his own children having the same sort of experiences. But I needed support too – I was pregnant, and working full-time, and doing most of the household stuff too. I didn't need a stressed-out person who I had to tiptoe around. It really drove a wedge between us, and now the baby is here, I'm not sure we'll ever get back to how we were before. He's still working late most nights."

Below are some more stories from the other side – a mother's perspective. They do give some insight into what partners of

depressed men are going through. They also really highlight
the need for action – in most of these cases nothing was ever
done about the man's attitude or behaviour, and so often
relationship difficulties will occur.

"We conceived really early on in our relationship – less than
a year after we started properly seeing each other, and it wasn't
planned. He was concerned, initially, and he was sometimes
quite against it, but we made the mutual decision to keep the
baby and we had a baby girl. She is now eighteen months'
old and things are terrible.

Things in our relationship really changed when the baby
arrived. The main problem at the start was to do with sleeping
arrangements – I wanted to have the baby sleep with me and
he wanted her to be in her own room. We tried the cot, but
it didn't work, so we had to go back to her sleeping in our
bed, because it was the easiest for all of us. But he got woken
up a lot when the baby was awake in the night, and he is
awful when he is tired; he got really irritated and angry with
the whole situation. He also got more and more snappy with
me, and was often nasty and critical. Sometimes he had
outbursts where he shouted at me that he hated our daughter.
He blames me entirely for this, mostly it is because it was my
'selfish' choice to co-sleep and I didn't stop when he said he
didn't want to. He would blame me and criticise me for
everything, saying that I don't love him – that I can't love him
because I have behaved so selfishly. I got tired of him saying
this all the time, so I tried to apologise and accept all the
blame – it made no difference.

He is usually the kind of person people really like, and so
it's so difficult to bear him like this as I feel like I have nobody
to talk to. To everyone else he is kind, selfless and
hardworking– he used to be like this with me. But I get his

other side most of the time now, which I have only ever seen when he's with me – he can be accusative, judgemental, nasty.

We are now at the stage where he will disappear for a few hours, leaving notes around the place which imply that he is leaving us for good, only to return a few hours later completely in denial that he was ever going anywhere. I told him to make a choice – to stay and work things out or to leave – I was getting so upset with the constant worry over our relationship and the stress of living with such a resentful person. Things haven't been properly resolved between us. There is no intimacy, and he hasn't made much effort with our daughter either. I don't know how long we can go on like this."

Anger can be a problem for depressed fathers:

My husband really has a problem with anger at the moment, and I'm sure it started after our daughter was born a few years ago. He used to be 'normal' – I never suspected he could be like this and I thought we had a fantastic and healthy relationship. We've been together about ten years, so I am really shocked that this has all happened now.

He started having problems less than a month after she was born. I thought it was just a case of him adjusting to life with a newborn, and I could understand that he was frustrated sometimes. It is difficult to change our routines so much, and to transition from being carefree to being parents, but I cannot deal with these aggressive outbursts of his any more. He has never hurt me, physically, but he does threaten it sometimes. He often kicks and breaks things around the house, and is never violent towards me or our daughter, but she is two now, and can see that Daddy is angry and is breaking things. The outbursts and so unpredictable – if I knew when he'd kick off I'd make sure we were away from him somewhere, but he can be fine for a while, and then he'll suddenly have three or four outbursts in a few weeks. I don't understand why he can't control himself.

He does acknowledge that he has a problem, and he knows it's not acceptable to do this in front of our daughter. He has looked at a few self-help books, but I think he needs to find the cause of the anger – he can't tell me. And maybe I should make him go to the GP and ask for some therapy session or something to try and deal with this before it gets worse."

"I am having serious problems with my marriage at the moment. We always wanted children, but due to some fertility issues (for both of us) we had to have IVF, and on the second try I got pregnant. It cost a lot of money, and was emotionally very difficult, but we were sure it was the best thing for us, and we desperately wanted a family. However, throughout the pregnancy, my husband was not at all interested in the baby. He wouldn't come to any appointments with me, and wouldn't listen when I was trying to tell him little things, wouldn't feel my bump when the baby kicked – little things, but they got me down. We had lots of other things going on though, like a house move, and he changed jobs just after we conceived, so I just put it down to general life stresses.

Our baby is now less than a month old, and since the beginning we have had problems. He hasn't slept in the same bed as me since I came home with the baby, saying that he couldn't cope with the crying. He sleeps on the sofa now; after a few nights of being woken up and getting angry he's decided he'll just sleep there for the time being. I don't think that's normal.

He's getting really angry, saying he's not cut out for this; he can't cope with the baby being around and can't cope with the tiredness. He mentioned leaving, and then I questioned him and he said maybe I should leave and take the baby with me.

I'm very concerned. He does have a history of being moody and wanting to have all the attention, but I'm not sure why he is surprised that my attention is elsewhere for now. What did he expect it would be like? We had discussed him becoming a full- time stay-at-home dad sometime in the future, but I think this is not going to be an option. If I ask him to leave I think he would not. He is very stubborn, and I'm worried about talking to him about this, and from past experience I know it will make things a whole lot worse. I can't tell my parents or friends about this. I'd hate to see my parents worry about me, and I don't even know how to bring it up with my friends. I mentioned it to my midwife, who is still visiting since the baby took a while to put on weight. She said I should get him to go to the GP to get help, but I know he won't."

"My husband has changed recently. He was always, and still sometimes is, such a lovely, warm, funny man, but recently he's become really angry and I feel like I'm treading on eggshells around him. He also says he no longer loves me, which is devastating, since I love him. We have two children, one of whom is less than three months' old, and I desperately want to stay together for their sakes. I come from a broken family, and I don't want that for my kids.

He says he still cares about me, and finds me attractive, but is no longer in love with me. He has always had a problem with my parenting style – thinking I was too focused on them and let my world revolve around them. I co-slept, breastfed, and carried them around in slings, but he felt that I no longer loved him because I had the children as my priority, and now he says he no longer loves me! We have barely had sex for the last year – a combination of a new baby, being pregnant, and having a toddler to care for – but I was always confident we'd get our sex life back on track."

Leslie writes about her husband's behaviour here. His use of pornography is damaging their relationship – it is a good example of how male behaviour is perceived by their partners, and it seems that in this case it is a reaction to his wife's pregnancy and the birth of their child.

"I knew he had watched porn in the past when I got together with him, and I know he did sometimes after we got married – I didn't care too much really. When I was pregnant he stopped trying to have sex with me, and I took it as a kind of blessing, since I was so tired a lot of the time. I didn't want to have sex either, but in hindsight I know that he was using porn most nights rather than coming to bed with me. It continued after the baby was born and after a while I got fed up and confronted him. He came up with a whole load of excuses, like how he thought I wasn't happy with my body after pregnancy and he didn't want to make me feel uncomfortable – which obviously made me feel worse! Things improved for a few months, but I am still on maternity leave and it seems like he watches porn at every available opportunity – whenever I leave the house, even when I am having a nap with the baby. If I try to talk to him about it he won't engage, just completely shuts down. I am not happy at the moment, but I can't make him see that."

Here, Michelle talks about her husband's drinking and how it affects her and her family.

"My husband works very hard, and I expect he does, but I don't count going out drinking nearly every night as work. We've got two children, aged four and six months, and about four or five times a week he will go out after work without telling me and just come home whenever he feels like it. If he does happen to tell me he's going out, he rarely sticks to the time he said he'd be back, and doesn't answer his phone, so I am left waiting for him for hours on end. Although he tells me he is 'networking', he fails to understand that I am stuck at home with a breastfeeding baby. The baby is quite difficult in the evenings, and often needs to be held until she goes to bed after ten o'clock, so I get no break, no one to talk to, and I feel really lonely and isolated."

Two other stories about excessive drinking around pregnancy and childbirth follow this story from Faye:

"We have just had our third child, who is a few months' old. We both enjoyed a drink when we first got together before we were married, but I have pretty much stopped since we had the children. My husband, however, goes out every week night 'marketing', which is really just going out and getting hammered with clients. I am finding it really difficult to deal with. He is out until after midnight most nights, and often he has gone on such a bender that I have woken up in the middle of the night to find him passed out on the sofa. I have three young children to look after. I don't think I can take much more."

"My husband's drinking is out of control. I stay at home all day looking after our three-year-old and I'm heavily pregnant with our second child, but he goes out drinking after work on a regular basis – often three or four times a week. He usually rolls in steaming after midnight, waking me up and pissing me off, since he always calls me earlier to promise he's on his way home – only to change his mind without telling me, and turns up hours later. I'm pretty sure he's not having an affair, and that it's only the going out drinking. We have awful rows about it, and after me crying hysterically he promises not to do it again, only for this ridiculous behaviour to start up again by the end of the week.

We can't afford counselling. I'm so worried that he'll do this once the new baby is here. As it is he doesn't spend much time with our first born – at the weekends he's always nursing a hangover, and then during the week he's out getting pissed and so misses bedtime. I do love him, and I know he loves me, but this drinking will tear our family apart."

"We planned this pregnancy together and were supportive of each other when it took us a few months to conceive, but now I am eighteen weeks' pregnant my partner's behaviour has changed and I hate it. He stays out late nearly every night, drinking and hanging out with his friends, and now has started being ridiculously irresponsible with our money too! He spends almost all his salary on himself and these drinking sessions, but we need to buy things for when the baby is here! I feel like I don't know who he is any more. He was so happy about the baby, but now I feel like he doesn't care because he's acting so strange."

A difficult pregnancy can also be a trigger for depression:

"I had a really difficult pregnancy and birth, and my husband was not supportive during either. We definitely aren't as close as we were before the baby arrived, but I thought things were getting better, as I've realised that if I want to avoid having yet another row, I will have to do all the housework and childcare.

Occasionally I ask him to do one tiny thing, like emptying the dishwasher, or changing a nappy, but more often than not he blows up, shouting that he works 'his arse off' and he doesn't want to be told to do 'housework' as well. He has never bathed our baby, or fed him since we have started weaning – I was breastfeeding exclusively, but now there are more opportunities for him to get involved and he just isn't interested. He sometimes wants to play with him, but that's it.

I had a really bad experience with the birth of our child, and he is really dismissive about it. I was telling a friend all about it the other day and he was there too. When she'd gone he said that my birth experience was completely normal and he didn't know what I was so upset about. I wish he was more understanding. I just don't feel like I can rely on him for any support.

We don't have any family that live near us. I looked into counselling, but we have nobody we could leave the baby with, and realistically I don't think he'd agree to it. Actually, I think I'd be opening a huge can of worms by going to counselling and I don't know if our marriage could survive it.

He sleeps in the spare room so that he gets a good night's sleep for work, but he's started doing it at weekends now too. I don't know how to address this without yet more rows."

Sometimes there is a history of depression:

"My husband was fine for a while after the birth. I was worried because he has suffered from depression in the past and a diagnosis of bi-polar disorder has been thrown around. He has been taking medication almost constantly for a few years now, but after our daughter was born he couldn't find time to exercise or have much time to himself, and so his symptoms escalated and he sunk into a major depression. He lies in bed a lot, and won't talk to me, but sometimes sits around crying too. He is also angry a lot of the time and I feel like he has a lot of resentment towards us, well, me and my daughter, just waiting below the surface. The atmosphere at home is so much better when he's not around, and I can't help worrying that it's going to affect our daughter and she'll pick up on it in some way.

I try to be supportive. I give him space when he needs it and try to listen to him talk about his feelings if he wants to, but sometimes I can't hold it together any more and I shout at him for making me cope with a husband like him. It always leads to the most terrible arguments. I don't want to make things worse for him, but I find it so hard to deal with him.

I've noticed that our daughter is getting very bad separation anxiety if she's away from me for even the briefest of moments, and recently she has been reaching for her dad and he has been turning away. It really breaks my heart. He also doesn't seem to have any compassion towards me any more. He doesn't tell me he loves me and he doesn't ever comfort me if he sees me crying."

There are often changes in behaviour during pregnancy and after childbirth – here are some experiences of women whose partners have had affairs:

"My husband got an offer to move to another part of the country for his job a few months before our son was born and we decided to accept it and move our family a few hundred miles away. We were supposed to be moving together, but when our son was a few weeks' old he decided to move on his own, and so I had ten weeks alone packing up our old house and dealing with a newborn. I later found out that he had asked his boss if he could start early, but he initially let me believe it was his boss's decision, not his. I was livid when I found out and I'm still hurt that he could leave us at such a vulnerable and exciting time. He didn't always come home at weekends either, and showed little interest in our son when we talked on the phone. He didn't seem to acknowledge how hard I was finding it being on my own.

We are together now, but I looked at his phone and he has been texting and calling a girl from work. I confronted him immediately and he told me it had been going ever since he started at the company. He said that everything changed when our son was born and there was no spark in our marriage any more. I think we will break up over this."

"We have been married for nearly ten years. Last year, when I was three months' pregnant with our second child, I found out that he had been unfaithful. He had been having an affair with another woman, which had started when our first child was under a year old – he says it went on for a few months, and this would have been when I was at home with the baby while on maternity leave. When he told me about the affair our marriage started to break apart, and we argued almost constantly. I was so scared about being on my own that I didn't want to leave him, and so he stayed and we argued. It was causing me so much stress and anguish that we decided to separate when I was six months' pregnant.

Before I gave birth he begged me to take him back and make a go of things. I was vulnerable and lonely, and wanted desperately to be a family unit, so I agreed, believing everything would be ok. Everything was alright for a few weeks, and then he suddenly announced that he didn't love me enough not to cheat on me again. I can't believe he did this when we had just welcomed our second child into the world."

"My husband and I had two babies within fifteen months – the second was totally unplanned, and it meant that I have had to cope for a long time with sleepless nights, breastfeeding, and the demands of two very young children. Our relationship started to disintegrate when I was pregnant for the second time. He would start picking fights and we were bickering almost constantly by the time the kids were one- and two-years-old.

After this had been going on for a while I found out that he had been having an affair with someone from work. He says it started when our second child was a couple of months old, but I think he had been seeing her before then, probably when I was pregnant.

Since I found out, he has left us, but still comes here twice a week to see the children. Before we had them he was a different person and I thought we had a great relationship. I can't believe he has done this to me, and without telling me how unhappy he was in the first place. I can't believe he just dumped all this on me and left."

Some experiences of mothers whose partners started to work long hours after their child was born:

"I was really worried about my boyfriend after the birth of our first child. I went to the GP to get some advice as I really didn't know where else to turn. He was fine during my pregnancy, excited even, but on the morning that we woke up for me to go to hospital to be induced, he ran to the bathroom to throw up. I thought nothing of it to be honest; I just thought he was as nervous as I was.

After the birth he just slept and slept, and didn't want to hold the baby at all once we were home. He'd make excuses if I asked him, and he *never* asked to hold her of his own accord. I had to force him to take her while I got things done, but I never got very far because he'd be trying to give her back as soon as he could, or would put her in her swing so he didn't have to hold her.

He also started working ridiculous hours, sometimes 4 a.m. until 9 or 10 p.m., but refused to get another job, saying he was happy with this one. He was getting angry with me that we didn't do as many things as we used to do; how we didn't go out, how he couldn't just do whatever he wanted any more. He would just go out without us, and didn't want to be with me and the baby at all. Some nights he would stay at his brother's house but not contact me to tell me, and I'd be up until the early hours trying to find out where he was. Once or twice I have caught him out and when he said he was at his brother's he was really out drinking with his friends.

He also lost a lot of weight since I gave birth, probably over a stone, and he looked totally different. I had heard him being sick in the mornings sometimes, and he refused to let me make him any lunch to take to work. He was also so irritable all the time, something he never was before the baby.

We did have a talk where he told me he was unhappy and had been for a few months, but he was really reluctant to put it all on the arrival of the baby and the fact that he'd become a dad. I suggested that it could be male post-partum depression, but he was really embarrassed and didn't want to admit to it. He still won't, and his behaviour has not changed. He is currently living mostly at his brother's house, unwilling to get help or to tell me what's wrong."

"We have a lovely nine-month-old daughter, but I feel like my marriage is breaking down. My husband is an accountant for a small firm, but he has been working increasingly long hours, leaving me alone every night, because he's often not home until one or two in the morning. He also works at least one whole day each weekend. I feel totally miserable, because after a full day with the baby I just want some adult company, and, really, would just like to spend some time with my husband.

He also does nothing around the house, and even though I've always been quite an independent person, I don't want to run the household by myself as well as look after a small baby. I've tried talking to him, and he is apologetic, even promising to spend a bit more time with us, but nothing ever changes. I'm getting really fed up with him never being here. He really doesn't know his own daughter well at all."

"When I was thirty-four weeks' pregnant with our second child I had to challenge my husband about his appalling behaviour. He had been distant for a good six months, and so I asked him what was going on – he told me he didn't love me any more, and hadn't for the last two years, since our first child was a year old.

We have had a tough few years. I was made redundant soon after the birth of our first child (who is now three) and I have been unemployed on and off since then, only managing to bring in a few hundred pounds per month. This has been financially very difficult, and he threw himself into his own work to make sure we were secure.

We tried counselling, but while he says he wants to leave and doesn't love me, he makes no moves to actually go. He says there isn't anyone else, but he is adamant that he is going to move out."

CHAPTER TWELVE

Conclusion – what can we do?

Postnatal depression in fathers is real. The symptoms may be different from those traditionally seen in mothers, but the feelings are there and can have long-lasting and damaging effects on fathers, their relationships, and their children. So what can we do?

The most important thing is to raise awareness. Mental illness retains much of the stigma it has always had, and unfortunately we don't talk about it much as a society. Things are getting better though, with many charities tirelessly campaigning to reduce the stigma, and more and more people becoming aware of the different illnesses and disorders that do exist. Postnatal depression has always been an area of discomfort, since a baby is supposed to bring happiness to a couple, and a mother is supposed to be happy and content. Women are victims of these preconceptions and of the subsequent silence when it comes to their own mental health, so there needs to be more acknowledgement of a mother's mental health as well as a father's.

Organisations such as the Fatherhood Institute can help to make sure fathers are treated more equally when it comes to maternity services, or at least make sure that they are not ignored. But really the change has to come from all of us. We all need to see fathers as emotional people who are also likely to struggle with parenting.

Equality in maternity and other community services will mean that we have to take steps to drop our fixation on essentialist gender roles. Parents should be seen as equals, regardless of how their gender has influenced their upbringing – outdated gender roles have cause many problems for fathers (and mothers).

We need to acknowledge that fathers need to be better prepared for childbirth and parenting – male-only ante-natal classes are becoming more common and we must encourage fathers to attend and take advantage of talking to other men in the same position.

We must also be aware of the signs of depression in men. As I have discussed extensively, and as can be seen in the many personal stories of postnatal depression in this book, a father's behaviour is the key indicator of his mood.

Talking about feelings can be difficult, but with every professional I have come across in researching this book, and in every study, it is advocated as something that can make a difference. Family members and friends should be aware that a new father might want to talk. The simple question "How are you feeling?" is easy to ask – health-care professionals should be aware too that it only takes one person asking this to make a father feel important.

GPs, online forums, counsellors and therapists are all good sources of support, should a father need it. They must be reminded of these options constantly.

Postnatal depression matters because it can be a possible trigger for domestic violence, divorce, or relationship breakdown. All this can be devastating for a child, and so we owe it to them to acknowledge paternal postnatal depression and to give ourselves the tools to deal with it.

ACKNOWLEDGEMENTS

First thanks have to go to my editor, Sarah Sibley, who certainly had her work cut out for her, but helped me make this book the best it could be. I would also like to thank everyone at Free Association Books for their unending support with this project.

Thank you to all those who contributed – in no particular order – Adam Jukes, Michel Odent, Barry Watt, Jeszemma Garratt and Andrew Solomon. It has been a privilege to talk to you, thank you for giving up your precious time to let me interview you or to send me an email.

Thanks to all those who contributed their own personal story – these will be invaluable to other sufferers.

Thanks to Brooke for the helpful discussions, feedback, opinions and all round solid support and friendship. Thanks to my Mum, for all the babysitting, which has allowed me to write uninterrupted. Thanks to all my friends who have taken an interest and given me their opinions, and who have been as excited about this book as I am.

For Robbie I reserve the biggest thanks. For everything. Always.

USEFUL LINKS AND GROUPS FOR SUFFERERS AND THEIR FAMILIES

postpartummen.com

mensdepression.org

daddynatal.co.uk
Antenatal classes and other workshops for men only.

postpartum.net
Postpartum Support International – based in Oregon, but a worldwide organisation.

recoveryispossible.co.uk
PSS PND Project – based in Liverpool

postpartumprogress.com

pni.org.uk

postnataldepression.com

birthtraumaassociation.org.uk

helpfordepression.com

mind.org.uk

sane.org.uk

fatherhoodinstitute.org

Acacia Family Support
acacia.org.uk
Raises awareness and provides support for families suffering
from pre and postnatal depression. Based in Birmingham.

Bluebellcare.org
Based in Bristol. A charity for mums, dads and families
affected by pre and postnatal depression.

The Marcé Society
marcesociety.com
Swansea based group dedicated to supporting research and
assistance surrounding prenatal and postpartum mental health.

Pandas
pandasfoundation.org.uk
Leading UK charity in supporting families suffering from
antenatal and postnatal illness.

Youngness.co.uk
Raising awareness of young mums and dads affected by PND.

REFERENCES

Abidin, R. R. (1976). *Parenting Stress Index* (Third Edition: Professional Manual). Odessa, FL: Psychological Assessment, 1995.

American Psychiatric Association. (2000). *Diagnostic and Statistical Manual of Mental Disorders DSM-IV-TR*. Washington, DC: American Psychiatric Press.

Bergström, M., Rudman, A., Waldenström, U., & Kieler, H. (2013). Fear of childbirth in expectant fathers, subsequent childbirth experience and impact of antenatal education: Subanalysis of results from a randomized controlled trial. *Acta Obstetricia et Gynecologica Scandinavica, 92:* 967–973.

Cox, J. L., Holden, J. M., & Sagovsky, R. (1987). Detection of postnatal depression: Development of the 10-item Edinburgh postnatal depression scale. *British Journal of Psychiatry, 150:* 782–786.

De Montigny, F., Girard, M. E., Lacharite, C., Dubeau, D., & Devault, A. (2013). Psychosocial factors associated with paternal postnatal depression. *Journal of Affective Disorders, 150:* 44–49.

Elander, J. & Rutter, M. (1996). Use and development of the Rutter parents' and teachers' scales. *International Journal of Methods in Psychiatric Research, 6*(2): 63–78.

Gawlik, S., Müller, M., Hoffmann, L. Dienes, A., Wallwiener, M., Sohn, C., Schlehe, B., & Reck, C. (2014). Prevalence of paternal perinatal depressiveness and its link to partnership satisfaction and birth concerns. *Archives of Women's Mental Health, 17*(1): 49–56.

Golding, J., Pembrey, M., & Jones, R. (2001). Avon longitudinal study of parents and children. *Paediatric and Perinatal Epidemiology, 15*(1): 74–87.

Goodman, R., Ford, T., Richards, H., Gatward, R., & Meltzer, H. (2000). The development and well-being assessment. *Journal of Child Psychology and Psychiatry, 41*(5): 537–655.

Habib, C., (2012). Paternal perinatal depression: An overview and suggestions towards an intervention model. *Journal of Family Studies 18*(1): 4–16.

Hanington, L., Heron, J., Stein, A., & Ramchandani, P. (2012). Parental depression and child outcomes – is marital conflict the missing link? *Child: Care, Health and Development, 38* (4): 520–529.

Jukes, A. (2010). *Is There a Cure for Masculinity?* London: Free Association Books.

Kim & Swain (2007) Sad dads: paternal postpartum depression *Psychiatry 2007 Feb, 4(2): 35-47*

Martin, C. R, (2012). *Perinatal Mental Health: A Clinical Guide.* Cumbria, UK: M&K Update.

McKay, K., Ross, L. R., & Goldberg, A. E. (2010). Adaptation to parenthood during the post-adoption period: A review of the literature. *Adoption Quarterly,* 13, 125-144.

Melrose, S. (2010). Paternal postpartum depression: How can nurses begin to help? *Contemporary Nurse, 34*(2): 199–210.

Naouri, A. (2005). *Fathers and Mothers* (Trans. G. R Edwards). London: Free Association Books.

Nyström, K., & Öhrling, K. (2004). Parenthood experiences during the child's first year: Literature review. *Journal of Advanced Nursing, 46*(3): 319–330.

Orbach, S., & Eichenbaum, L. (1983). *What Do Women Want?* London: Harper Collins, 2000.

Premberg, A., Hellström, A. L., & Berg, M. (2008). Experiences of the first year of as father. *Scandinavian Journal of Caring Sciences, 22*: 56–63.

Ramchandani, P., O'Connor, T. G., Evans, J., Heron, J., Murray. L., & Stein, A. (2008). The effects of pre- and postnatal depression in fathers: A natural experiment comparing the effects of exposure to depression on offspring. *The Journal of Child Psychology and Psychiatry, 49*(10): 1069–107.

Ramchandani, P., Psychogiou, L., Vlachos, H., Iles, J., Sethna, V., Netsi, E., & Lodder, A. (2011). Paternal depression: An examination of its links with father, child and family functioning in the postnatal period. *Depression and Anxiety, 28:* 471–477.

Ramchandani, P., Stein, A., Evans, J., O'Connor, T. G., & the ALSPC study team. (2005). Paternal depression in the postnatal period and child development: A prospective population study. *The Lancet, 365*: 2201–2205.

Reece, S. M. (1992). The parent expectations survey: A measure of perceived self-efficacy. *Clinical Nursing Research, 1*(4): 336–346.

Spanier, G. B. (1976). Measuring dyadic adjustment: New scales for assessing quality and marriage. *Journal of Family and Marriage, 38*: 15–28.

Tew, M. (1998). *Safer Childbirth*. London: Free Association Books.

Tohotoa, J., Maycock, B., Hauck, Y. L, Dhaliwal, S. Howat, P., Burns, S., & Binns, C. W. (2012). Can father inclusive practice reduce paternal postnatal anxiety? A repeated measures cohort study using the hospital anxiety and depression scale. *BMC Pregnancy and Childbirth, 12*: 75.

Weinstock 1996; Gluckman et al. 2005; Levine 2005; Connor et al. 2005.

Parental depression and child outcomes – is marital conflict the missing link? *Childcare, Health and Development July 2012, 38(4): 520-529*

Zierau, F., Bille, A., Rutz, W., & Bech, P. (2002). Gotland male
    depression scale. *Nordic journal of psychiatry, 56*(4): 265–271.
Zigmond, A. S., & Snaith, R. P. (1983). The hospital anxiety and
    depression scale. *Acta Psychiatrica Scandinavica, 67*(6): 361–370.